Esteeming the Gift
Of a Pastor

A Handbook for Christians
Who Want To Grow Up in God

By

Judy Wilder

Esteeming the Gift of a Pastor:
A Handbook for Christians
Who Want To Grow Up in God
By Judy Wilder
ISBN 0-615-11694-9
Copyright © 2000 by Judy Wilder
1718 Garfield Ave.
Aurora, IL 60506

Editorial Consultant: Cynthia Hansen
Cover Design: Greg Lane, Inspired Graphics
Text Design: Lisa Simpson, Words Unlimited

Dedication

I dedicate this book to my husband George, who has been such a loving support to me over the years. No matter what crazy dream I pursue, George never gives me a hard time. Even after I pick myself up from a failed attempt and get ready to pursue my next dream, he is always right there in my corner, rooting for me. I thank God for giving me such a wonderful husband!

Table of Contents

Acknowledgments

I would like to thank several people who were instrumental in the writing of this book. First, I would like to thank three very special couples:

- Pastor Dick and Lynne Pakenham of Vineyard Community Church in Naperville, Illinois. Dick and Lynne faithfully pastored my husband and me for ten years.

- Pastor Dan and Gayle Haas of Aurora Community Church in Aurora, Illinois. Dan was also the administrator of Covenant Christian School, where I served as the school nurse for three years.

- My current pastors, Jeff and Christine Miller of Abundant Life Family Church. Jeff and Christine were very supportive of this project, and Pastor Jeff's counsel was invaluable in putting this book together.

These couples are all excellent role models of godly pastors. Although they are not perfect people (and do not pretend to be), they have given their lives to shepherd the people Jesus has assigned to them. All three of these couples have withstood opposition and persecution. Yet through it all, they have remained totally committed to God's call on their lives. They have not and they will not quit. Therefore, they stand as examples of integrity, honor, and total commitment.

I also wish to thank Rev. Wanda Casper, director of *Light of the World Ministries*. In the summer of 1999, I poured out my heart to her concerning the dishonor most pastors receive from their congregations. She told me that I had to write a book about the subject — so I did!

Foreword

The book you hold in your hand is controversial and dangerous. It is controversial because it goes against the grain of religious tradition; dangerous because it has the potential to revolutionize your walk of faith.

If you desire to grow up in God and receive His best for your life, read on with an open heart. You will never be the same. If you are content to live an average Christian life, don't even bother reading the book, for you will only be offended. Be forewarned — lukewarm Christians will have a difficult time receiving the truths contained in *Esteeming the Gift of a Pastor*.

This book reveals that a true pastor is more than a feeder. He is a leader equipped by the Holy Spirit to shepherd the flock of God.

Outside of your immediate family, no other person is more important to your life than your pastor. Why? Jesus chose your pastor to be your shepherd. Sheep need a shepherd, and all believers are sheep. Without your shepherd, you will never become all God has destined you to be. In this book, you will learn how to recognize, receive, and take care of the gift you have received from Jesus Christ.

I am persuaded that all believers will greatly benefit from the principles in this book. Pastors, elders, deacons, and other church leaders should be required to read *Esteeming the Gift of a Pastor*. My prayer is that it finds wide acceptance in the Body of Christ and brings blessing to multitudes of churches, pastors, and their families. I am of the opinion that the Church in these last days desperately needs to receive these truths before the end-time harvest can come in.

Judy and her husband George have been faithful members of Abundant Life Family Church for three years. It has been a joy to be their pastor. Before coming to our church, they were faithful members of Vineyard Community Church in Naperville, Illinois, for ten years. They have lived by the truths contained in this book.

Judy is not a Bible teacher or a minister; she is a committed believer with a revelation from God. As her pastor, I believe she has obeyed the Holy Spirit in writing this book. May God speak to you as you read *Esteeming the Gift of a Pastor*.

Obey them that have the rule over you, and submit yourselves: for they watch for your souls, as they that must give account, that they may do it with joy, and not with grief: for that is unprofitable for you.

Hebrews 13:17 *KJV*

Jeff Miller, Pastor
Abundant Life Family Church
Aurora, Illinois

Preface

I have four main purposes for writing this book:

First, I want to encourage pastors with the knowledge of who the Bible says they are.

Second, I want to encourage all the "sheep" who love and honor their pastors. So often these same people shake their heads in unbelief as friends leave their churches over offenses and resentments toward the same pastor whom they love and esteem.

Third, I pray that this book convicts church-hoppers and troublemakers in the local church and convinces them to change their ways.

Finally, dear reader, if you don't know yet just how important the role of your pastor is in your life, I want to reveal that to you in this book. I want you to gain a new appreciation and esteem for this priceless ministry gift, given by the Head of the Church for the benefit of the Body of Christ — given for the benefit of *you*.

Chapter 1
Laying the Foundation

But when He [Jesus] saw the multitudes, He was moved with compassion for them, because they were weary and scattered, like sheep having no shepherd.

— Matthew 9:36

Of the many blessings God provides for us in this life, some of the most important come in human form. God delights in using His people to bless His people. Never was this more true than when Jesus ascended on High and gave gifts unto men — the fivefold ministry offices of apostle, prophet, evangelist, pastor, and teacher (Eph. 4:10-11).

Of these five ministry offices, the pastor is the most personal gift that Jesus gives to His people. Jesus not only gives every believer a pastor, He also associates tremendous blessings with receiving this ministry gift. Too often, however, believers have problems accepting this gift.

I want to show you how to recognize and honor your pastor so you can receive the full benefits of this personal gift from Jesus to you. But first, let's build a foundation, beginning with some important, basic information. Without an understanding of these basic principles, the role of the pastor makes no sense.

Relearning God's Ways

Our God is the Creator and Lord of the universe. He controls it all. In Genesis 1:28, He gave Adam authority over the earth. Later, when Adam and Eve rebelled against God, Adam's authority was transferred to Satan, and Satan became the god of this world (2 Cor. 4:4).

We can see Satan's position of authority when he tempted Jesus in the wilderness, offering Him the kingdoms of the world. Satan stated clearly, *"...All this power will I give thee, and the glory of them: for that is delivered unto me; and to whomsoever I will I give it"* (Luke 4:6 *KJV*). Significantly, Jesus didn't dispute Satan's claim.

When we accept Jesus as our Lord and Savior, we are born again. We die spiritually to this world (Satan's domain), and our spirits are reborn to the Kingdom of God (*see* John 3:1-21). We are now spiritually alive unto God; our spirits are joined to His Kingdom. However, our minds still have to be renewed to His Kingdom, which operates differently from the world (Rom. 12:2). We have to learn *God's* ways.

A Part of God's Larger Plan

An important aspect of learning God's ways is learning how to function as members of a larger Body of believers. You see, God has always had a plan for mankind, and He works through His people — willing, obedient vessels who know how to hear His voice and take their place as a part of His larger plan.

In order to fulfill our God-ordained role in the Body of Christ, we must first understand that God relates to His creation on several different levels. First, He relates to us as *individuals*. Jesus is our personal Savior and Lord. He has a plan for each of our individual lives. Proverbs 16:9 (*KJV*) says, *"A man's heart deviseth his way: but the Lord directeth his steps."*

God also has plans for *families*. For instance, the history of Israel is a history of Abraham's family. Even Jesus was a part of that genealogy. He was of the family (house) of David. David was of the tribe of Judah, and Judah was a great grandson of Abraham.

God also recognizes and relates to *nations*. In fact, the Bible is riddled with God's dealings with nations. Revelation 21:24 (*KJV*) says, *"And the nations of them which are saved shall walk in the light of it: and the kings of the earth do bring their glory and honour into it."*

Finally, Jesus has a plan for His *Church*. He speaks specifically to churches in the first four chapters of Revelation, and throughout the epistles, the Church is referred to as His Body.

Despite God's multi-dimensional relationship with His people, too many believers only relate to Him as individuals, acting as "lone rangers" in the Body of Christ. But in doing so, they limit themselves to only one aspect of God's plan, which is selfish and spiritually immature.

Jesus, the Head of the Church, hasn't left us without aid as we learn how to take our place in the Body of Christ. To help us, He has given ministry gifts. Ephesians 4:8-16 describes these ministry gifts, where they came from, and what their purpose is. This passage of Scripture especially examines the implications of receiving or not receiving these gifts.

Since all the ministry gifts come from Jesus (Eph. 4:10-11), they are therefore all very important to us as individual believers. The pastor is of particular importance. The word "pastor" means *shepherd*. In John 10:11, Jesus referred to Himself as the "Good Shepherd." Then in Matthew 9:36 (*KJV*), He looked at the multitudes who followed Him and *"...was moved with compassion on them, because they fainted, and were scattered abroad, as sheep having no shepherd."* It is obvious that God considers the role of a shepherd, or a pastor, of supreme importance to His people.

'Cult' or Godly Pastoral Leadership?

Before I go into detail about the role of a pastor in the Body of Christ, I want to confront an area of concern among believers. Many believers fear churches with strong commitment messages. They mistrust churches where the pastor actually runs the church and preaches about tithing and giving offerings. Malachi 3:8 ("Will a man rob God?") is often an unpopular verse with this type of Christian.

These believers fear they will somehow become involved in a cult. To them, the concept of "receiving a pastor" is equivalent to mind control. They imagine themselves ending up in a jungle drinking poison juice!

Actually, there is no clear definition of the word "cult." The *Oxford American Dictionary* defines a cult as *a system of religious worship; devotion to or admiration of a person or thing.*[1] By this definition, all churches that preach commitment to Jesus could be defined as cults!

Compton's Online Encyclopedia has a narrower view:

> Cult, a system of religious belief and practice; in late 20th century term often used to describe religious movements outside of the mainstream.... Usually these authoritative sects are accused of recruiting members through aggressive tactics such as manipulation or so-called "brainwashing," often taking advantage of weak, credulous or alienated youths; fund-raising and proselytizing are often major responsibilities of members.[2]

---

[1] Gordon Carruth, Eugene Ehrlich, Stuart Berg Flexner, Joyce M. Hawkins, *Oxford American Dictionary* (New York: Avon Books, 1980), p. 208.

[2] "Cult" article in *Compton's Online Encyclopedia*, v3.0 (El Segundo, California: The Learning Company, Inc.; Mattel, 1999), comptonsv3.web@aol.com.

Christians further limit the definition when they define a cult as a church that denies the divinity of Jesus. If a person couldn't get "born again" by adhering to the doctrine of a particular church, then that church is a cult. Thus, the whole issue of what constitutes a cult is very confusing.

Here are some characteristics of questionable churches or religious groups:

1. *Any church that exalts an earthly leader above Jesus.* Pastors exalt Jesus. They encourage believers to develop their own relationship with God.

2. *Any church that tries to control specific aspects of the members' lives.* God gave each of His children a free will. Therefore, pastors equip Christians to apply biblical principles to their everyday lives, leaving the believers to make their own decisions about the details of their lives. Pastors are also available to advise and counsel as needed.

3. *Any church that tries to isolate its members and discourage contact with family and friends.* Pastors encourage healthy family relationships. They also encourage their congregation to pray for their family members and friends because Jesus commanded believers to share the Gospel with *everyone*.

4. *Any church that teaches that the end justifies the means.* Pastors are more concerned with *how* a goal is reached. Sacrificing Christian principles is never acceptable. And if an activity is immoral, it is also unacceptable.

5. The same is true for any activity that is illegal — with one specific exception. Believers are not required to keep civil laws that forbid the practice of their faith. Believers have the inherent right to worship God, own or read the Bible, and tell others about Jesus. Therefore, scriptural pastors always encourage believers to worship God, read the Word, and share their faith.

6. *Any church that uses sleep deprivation, drugs, or hypnosis.* Godly pastors use only the Word of God to fulfill their scriptural mandate to preach, teach, correct, and lead.

Hebrews 12:6-8 states that godly correction is both necessary and beneficial:

For whom the Lord loves He chastens, and scourges every son whom He receives.

If you endure chastening, God deals with you as with sons; for what son is there whom a father does not chasten?

But if you are without chastening of which all have become partakers, then you are illegitimate and not sons.

According to *Vine's Expository Dictionary of New Testament Words,* the word "chasten" is the Greek word *paideuo,* meaning in a broad sense *training children; discipline; correction.*[3] God says that He chastens His children out of His love for them. Yet many believers tend to get very upset over being corrected. As soon as their pastor tries to correct them, they start yelling "cult" and accusing the pastor of abusing the

---

[3] W. E. Vine, M.A., *An Expository Dictionary of New Testament Words* (Old Tappan, New Jersey: Fleming H. Revell Co., 1966), p. 183-184.

sheep. But part of a pastor's job is to confront, correct, and rebuke members of his congregation when necessary. Pastors are to perfect the saints.

Churches with strong pastoral leadership can be wrongfully labeled cults. There are important differences. Godly pastors don't expect believers to park their brains at the door. They don't raise themselves up to be the messiah. However, they do preach the uncompromised Word of God and expect believers to make necessary changes in their lives.

So with that in mind, let's look in the Word to discover how God views the pastoral ministry gift. Jesus has given us this priceless gift to bless us and help bring us to spiritual maturity. But if we are to enjoy the full benefits of that gift, we must learn how to *receive, esteem,* and *honor* our pastor's God-ordained role in our lives.

Chapter 2
Accepting or Rejecting Our Gift

And they were offended in him. But Jesus said unto them, A prophet is not without honour, save in his own country, and in his own house.

And he did not many mighty works there because of their unbelief.

— Matthew 13:57-58 *KJV*

Something has changed in the Body of Christ since I got saved more than twenty-five years ago. I remember the first church I attended. There were so many new believers — so many people just waiting to be saved. They were so excited about finding Jesus. They'd sit through a three- or four-hour service, just waiting for the altar call. When the altar call was given, they'd jump up and actually *want* to walk down the aisle. They could hardly wait to give their hearts to Jesus.

As new believers, we eagerly followed our pastor, esteeming him as a gift from God. After all, he was a very special person. He had unlocked the way to abundant life for us!

We could hardly stand the wait between church services. Sunday night to Wednesday night seemed like an eternity. We read our Bibles and walked in the light we had, soaking up the pastor's teaching like sponges.

My church wasn't the exception back then; it was more the rule. But somewhere along the road, things changed.

Today pastors are often not allowed to lead the local church. They have to beg "mature Christians" to come to church. They initiate small groups at their own peril because small group leaders can challenge their authority. Church boards remind pastors that they'll never get rich in the ministry and warn them not to talk about money. Pastors are cautioned about making friends inside their own congregations because their church members could turn on them at any time.

The Way Jesus Organized His Kingdom

What happened? This isn't what Jesus had in mind for the local church. Ephesians 4 presents the leadership structure Jesus established for His Church. The *Amplified Version* states it very clearly in verse 8: *"Therefore it is said, When He ascended on high, He led captivity captive [He led a train of vanquished foes] and HE BESTOWED GIFTS ON MEN."*

In the Old Covenant, God worked through individuals. But when Jesus ascended on High, all that changed. He gave men and women as gifts to the Body of Christ to preach, teach, pastor, and direct His followers in reaching the world for His Kingdom. As mentioned earlier, we call these gifts "the fivefold ministry gifts." They include the apostle, the prophet, the evangelist, the pastor, and the teacher. Verse 11 (*AMP*) says "And His gifts were [varied; He Himself appointed and gave men to us]...some pastors (shepherds of His flock)...."

God wants us to have a personal relationship with Him as He leads us in our daily lives. He also wants us to take our place in His disciplined, committed army of followers. In this spiritual army, God has appointed the ministry gifts as His "officers." Since He appointed the ministry gifts, they carry His authority. That means He requires that we submit to the leadership of the gifts.

You see, Jesus is not interested in spiritual "lone rangers." He wants believers to follow the ministry gifts He has appointed as His leaders in the Church.

Jesus' purpose for giving these God-ordained ministry gifts is found in Ephesians 4:12-13 (*AMP*).

His intention was the perfecting and full equipping of the saints (His consecrated people), [that they should do] the work of ministering toward building up Christ's body (the church).

[That it might develop] until we all attain oneness in the faith and in the comprehension of the [full and accurate] knowledge of the Son of God, that [we might arrive] at really mature manhood (the completeness of personality which is nothing less than the standard height of Christ's own perfection), the measure of the stature of the fullness of the Christ and the completeness found in Him.

Paul continues to develop Jesus' purpose for giving the ministry gifts in verse 14. These gifts are to keep us stable and safe from false doctrine *"that we should no longer be children, tossed to and fro and carried about with every wind of doctrine, by the trickery of men, in the cunning craftiness of deceitful plotting."*

In other words, God provides believers with protection through the care and spiritual authority of the ministry gifts. Jesus also gave us the ministry gifts to perfect and equip us to minister to the lost and to build up the Body of Christ, the Church. There is a strong implication in these verses that without the ministry gifts, the fullness of Jesus' plan for us will not be attained.

All five of the ministry gifts are essential. Without any one of the gifts, the believer is incomplete. But every believer especially needs a pastor to find that place of spiritual protection, to reach maturity in Christ, and to fulfill God's plan for his or her life.

Accepting Our Gift

The word for gift in Ephesians 4:8 is *doma*. It indicates that the character of the gift is important.[4] Character is the sum of the qualities that makes a person who he or she is. In the same way, the ministry gifts are important because of who *they* are.

The men and women God appoints to these ministry offices are the actual gifts given to the Church. But what makes them who they are? That's the important part to understand.

It is God's *anointing* that makes the fivefold ministry offices what they are. They are supernatural gifts, empowered by the Holy Spirit. You see, when Jesus appoints men and women to be ministry gifts, He equips them supernaturally to fulfill their office.

Also, notice in Ephesians 4:11 that Jesus gave the pastor *to men* — He didn't give or call a person to a *church*. Many Christians are looking for a church home when they should be seeking the gift of a pastor.

We'll discuss more on recognizing and esteeming this particular ministry gift later. But the point I'm making here is that Jesus gives us the gift, and that gift is a *person*, equipped by Jesus to minister to us supernaturally. The pastor is equipped to mature us, to bring us into oneness within the local church, and to make us stable in the truth of God.

---

[4] W. E. Vine, M.A., *An Expository Dictionary of New Testament Words*, Vol. 2 (Old Tappan, New Jersey: Fleming H. Revell Co., 1966), p. 147.

Think how you would feel if Jesus came walking into your living room with your pastor at His side. Then suppose He began talking to you about your pastor.

"I have a gift for you," Jesus might say. "This is your pastor, My personal choice for you. This man knows just what you need. He will help you be all you can be. If you follow him, I can use you to reach this dying world.

"So many people are rushing headlong to hell. You can reach them if you follow this man. Whenever you can't hear Me clearly, he'll help you recognize the truth. With his help, you can stay in My perfect will."

Would you excitedly accept the gift? Would you begin your journey toward becoming all God created you to be? Or would you politely say, "No, thank You, Jesus. I'm saved. I'm not going to hell. That's enough for me. I can handle things from here"?

The desire of every one of us who are Christians is to know, love, and serve God. We want to love God with our whole heart, soul, mind, and strength. We want to be like Jesus, conformed to His image.

Well, a pastor is called to help us reach these goals. So how can we refuse this gift of God?

Rejecting Our Gift

Over the years, my husband and I have watched various pastors interact with congregations. We have seen pastors judged, slandered, manipulated, and abused. We have seen them grieved and their families devastated. One pastor's teenagers were so hurt, they stopped going to church. These children loved God and were on fire for Jesus. The betrayal of their trust was devastating.

Why is it so difficult for some people to receive a pastor?

For one thing, those of us who live in America are taught to be independent. We want to do things *our* way. We are taught to evaluate and criticize everything. As a people, we are also often undisciplined. We don't want to be told what to do.

The pastor is the only ministry gift to whom people are personally accountable. The other ministry gifts are vitally important. However, people have very little accountability with television ministries. If they don't like the minister's message, they just switch the channel. They may order the minister's tapes, videos, and books. But who holds them accountable for that information?

The other ministry gifts recognize the believer's need for a pastor. For example, many people receive Jesus in evangelistic meetings. But if they don't get hooked up with a pastor, they never grow. The evangelist has to move on to the next meeting. Therefore, many evangelists work as partners with local churches, trying to steer new believers into good churches within the community.

Pastors minister to their flock week in and week out. They give the people counsel, teaching, and personal ministry. Pastors expect to see changes. They expect to see their congregation growing in spiritual maturity and walking in the light they have. Pastors want to see the "measure of the stature of the fullness of Christ" in the lives of their congregation. But too often, people don't like to be held accountable.

Our pastor only counsels regular church attenders. Many people consider this mean and uncaring. They want counseling, but they don't want to be held accountable to their responsibility to commit themselves to a local church. Other people who are in financial difficulty often refuse to tithe. They want pastoral counseling without cost.

We want to pick the areas God can change, but that isn't the way it works. God confronts us with what *He* wants to see changed in our lives.

One day my husband and I had an interesting conversation with one of our acquaintances who was looking for a different church. When we told him about our church, he explained to us about his relationship with his current pastor. He said that he really held his pastor to accountability; he didn't just accept everything his pastor said. In this man's words, he "really gave the pastor a hard time." He seemed so proud of his treatment of his pastor.

Well, our pastor doesn't need anyone else giving him a hard time. We never again invited this man to church. His attitude represented the arrogance and disrespect of many Christians, and we weren't interested in giving our pastor an extra dose of it!

Even Matthew 18:15 (*NIV*) has been used to bash pastors: *"If your brother sins against you, go and show him his fault, just between the two of you. If he listens to you, you have won your brother over."*

But what constitutes sin? Certainly violating one of the Ten Commandments is sin. The problem is, people start labeling pastoral correction as sin because they feel the Holy Spirit's conviction but don't want to change. So their feelings get hurt, or they get offended at the pastor and want to go straighten him out!

Believers who react like that to correction are self-deceived. Over and over again, the Bible tells us that we must learn to receive correction and obey, even when it's hard on our flesh. Jesus said that even as He always kept His Father's commandments, God also gives us personal, individual instructions to obey: *"If ye keep my commandments, ye shall abide in my love; even as I have kept my Father's commandments, and abide in his love"* (John 15:10 *KJV*). And often those divine instructions come through our pastor!

A man once told my husband and me that God had spoken to him, telling him that our pastor was abusing the sheep. The man said God had instructed him to go to the pastor and bring him to repentance. No, I don't think so!

It's a serious matter when a pastor is found to be violating the Ten Commandments. But even in this situation, the principle set forth in Matthew 18:15 doesn't give anyone license to gossip about the pastor's sin. Jesus said we are to talk to the person who has sinned *privately*. That means the entire situation is private. No one else has to know. Talking about it is gossip, and it is sin.

Remember David and King Saul? David refused to hurt Saul. He would not touch God's anointed (1 Sam. 24:6-7).

Believers really show where their hearts and faith are when they gossip. They obviously don't believe that prayer changes anything. A mature Christian would be on his knees interceding rather than gossiping about the problem with others.

A friend of mine accused her pastor of being "so carnal." As I listened to her, I remembered Matthew 12:36 (*KJV*): *"But I say unto you, That every idle word that men shall speak, they shall give account thereof in the day of judgment."* The word "idle" means *fruitless or empty*.[5] If we will have to give account for all our fruitless, empty words, how much more judgment will we incur for speaking hurtful, damaging words about a person given as a gift to believers?

The Testing of Our 'Fruit'

Christians sometimes complain that their pastors don't appreciate their efforts. Their pastors don't pass around enough "please's" and "thank you's" and so are accused of "not walking in love."

But pastors are supposed to equip an army. They are to bring their congregation into oneness in the faith and help them grow to spiritual maturity. Their service to the local body is to be as unto the Lord, not according to the carnal whims and opinions of individual church members. Hebrews 11:6 says God is the Rewarder of those who diligently seek *Him*.

Sometimes people are offended by the way the pastor equips his flock. But God doesn't always teach by lecture (although He does give open-Book tests!). He tends to teach by putting us in challenging situations (*not* including sickness, disease, or poverty); then He tests us to see how we handle those situations. Someone once said that we find out what kind of fruit we are bearing in our lives when we're squeezed by circumstances. Well, sometimes God "squeezes us" through our pastor to test our fruit!

I have seen talented, gifted people come into a church and declare absolutely that God led them there. These people present themselves as "mature" Christians, but they soon become offended. Perhaps they feel they haven't been recognized quickly enough. Promotion to a leadership position doesn't

---

[5] Ibid., p. 243.

come quickly enough. Or maybe the pastor won't follow their sound advice. Maybe he isn't as sophisticated as they are or doesn't have the college credentials they have. One way or the other, something always seems to happen.

These gifted and powerful people are used to being listened to. So they compare their current church experience with past experiences and blame their present pastor for any undesirable discrepancies. Judging the pastor's weaknesses by their own strengths, they begin to see themselves as above him. Finally, they decide they can't submit to him.

Whatever the issue, the outcome is usually the same: Suddenly these people make the announcement that God is leading them to another church. This makes God sound unstable and unable to make up His mind.

No, God is the God who changes not (Mal. 3:6). Those dear Christians just flunked their test!

God's test has two questions:

1. Can you humble yourself and submit to the spiritual authority I have placed over you?

2. Does your "maturity" include the ability to walk in love — to forgive and not keep a record of wrongs?

God doesn't measure maturity in years. God's standard for maturity is the degree to which Christ has been formed in us.

So these talented Christians move on to another church. But they will take the same test again and again until they finally pass it.

Following Our Spiritual Coach

Jesus is our Example. Through His life, we see that spiritual maturity is demonstrated through humble and obedient submission. In intense anguish of heart, Jesus sweat drops of blood as He prayed in the Garden of Gethsemane. Nevertheless, He submitted Himself to the will of the Father, saying, "Not My will, but Yours be done" (Luke 22:41-44).

Similarly, our journey toward spiritual maturity begins when we accept the pastor God gives us. Does that mean we are always to follow our pastor? Yes, although there are three exceptions to that rule. We are not to follow any man that requires us to do something *illegal*, *immoral*, or *unscriptural*. Otherwise, we are to follow our pastor.

At times our pastor has asked my husband and me to do things that were inconvenient. Sometimes he has asked us to do something we didn't want to do. But so far, we haven't sweat any blood over the requests of our pastor!

I've heard Christians say, "The pastor just missed it on that decision." I've also heard, "It's the wrong timing for what the pastor has proposed for the church." Believers often think God has spoken to them about a decision the pastor has made, even though what they "heard" opposes the pastor. Why do they so quickly assume the pastor is wrong when he is the God-appointed authority responsible for making that decision? God is fully able to correct the pastor He has placed in authority over a local church.

That isn't to say we can't share our opinion with the pastor privately. Most pastors will listen to their church members' concerns. But ultimately, the pastor makes the final decisions.

He also takes the responsibility for those decisions, knowing he is accountable to God.

Obedience is often doing something we do not want to do. It's saying "yes" when we want to say "no."

Think of yourself as an aspiring Olympic athlete. With all your heart, you want that gold metal. You know that a wonderful coach lives in town, but you decide you can train on your own. You'll read books, listen to training tapes, and go to short-term training camps. You decide that should be enough.

No potential Olympic athlete in his right mind would do that! He would go to the best coach and do exactly what he said. That athlete would train until he couldn't move without pain. Then when his coach yelled at him to keep going, he would get up and do it all over again!

Shouldn't following Jesus' commandments deserve just as much commitment? Jesus commanded us to reach the lost. At stake is whether or not millions of people spend eternity in hell. And it is our pastors — our spiritual "coaches" — to whom Jesus gives His plan to reach those multitudes with the Good News that they can be saved.

Recognizing the 'Gideon' In Our Midst

One of my favorite Bible stories is the story of Gideon (Judges 6-8). Gideon looked like a coward, but the angel who visited him called him a mighty man of fearless courage (Judges 6:12). Gideon followed God when it wasn't comfortable, and the people followed Gideon because God was with him. Gideon had faith in God, so God used him to save Israel.

God honors faith. We have what we say with our mouths and believe in our hearts.

Jesus has called men to be pastors who shepherd and equip His flock. Jesus wants His people equipped for service (Eph. 4:12). Therefore, we need to begin seeing our pastor as a Gideon. We have to see who he is in God and stop focusing on the natural — to recognize and follow the anointing upon his life to stand in that office.

We say we have faith that the Bible is true. But the entire Bible is true — not just the parts we want to obey. Therefore, whether or not our flesh wants to submit to pastoral leadership, we have to acknowledge that, according to the Word, we have been given a gift from Jesus in the form of a pastor.

Our pastor is just a man, but Jesus appointed him and anointed him as a gift to a local body of believers. The supernatural gift of pastoring is operating in his life.

What we believe in life is eventually what we get. In the same way, what we believe about our pastor is what we will receive. If we focus only on our pastor's natural charisma, we will be disappointed. But if we look to him for supernatural pastoring, that is what we will receive.

Jesus could do no mighty works in His hometown because the people of Nazareth thought they knew Him and His family. They couldn't believe He was anyone special; therefore, they couldn't receive from Him.

Today our churches are filled with needy people. There are sick people who should be walking in divine health. There are tithers and givers who are barely making ends meet. Why aren't these believers abounding with more than enough the way God intended?

Often the reason people miss out on God's blessings is that they don't believe their pastor is anyone special. They only see the person who mows his lawn on Monday instead of the person who is their gift from Jesus. Thus, their own lack of esteem for their pastor shuts down the anointing on his life to help them.

But the Bible says God found Gideon *hiding*. Nevertheless, God used Gideon to save Israel, and He will use our pastors to accomplish His goals. All we have to do is receive the gift He's given us.

Personally, I am not in full-time ministry. I am a regular rank-and-file Christian. I basically do whatever the pastor asks me to do. Nevertheless, I write this book in a heartfelt attempt to help correct the pathetic condition of many churches. So many churches have been rendered powerless by constant infighting between pastor and church members. Pastors are trying to lead people who don't want to follow.

Jesus is the Lord of the universe. He is the precious Savior who died for us. He wants to bring all men into right relationship with Him. To aid in that divine goal, He gave gifts unto men — precious gifts from the hands of Jesus. These wonderful gifts are designed to form His image in us, to lead us and equip us.

But how do people treat their gift of a pastor? Many won't accept their pastor because they don't think they need one. Others emotionally bludgeon their pastor until he leaves the ministry or dies early. In either case, Jesus can do no mighty works in the midst of the people because of their unbelief.

Chapter 3
Be Ye Not Conformed to the World

And do not be conformed to this world, but be trans-
formed by the renewing of your mind, that you may
prove what is that good and acceptable and perfect will
of God.

— Romans 12:2

As we learn more of God's ways, we must always keep in
mind that the ways of this world are not the ways of God's
Kingdom. For example, God has a very definite structure of
authority in His Kingdom. Jesus is the Chief Shepherd (1 Peter
5:4), but He has always had "undershepherds" to lead His people. In the Old Testament, God used Israel to fulfill His will. In
the New Testament, God uses His Church, the Body of Christ.

The work of spreading the Gospel is given to the Church at
large. However, believers are to work to fulfill that divine mandate through the local church under the direction of the pastor.
The pastor is the head, or the undershepherd, of the local
church, operating under the authority of the Chief Shepherd,
Jesus.

First Peter 5:1-4 speaks to pastors about their responsibility
to the believers under their care:

> **The elders who are among you I exhort, I who**
> **am a fellow elder and a witness of the sufferings of**
> **Christ, and also a partaker of the glory that will be**
> **revealed:**
> **Shepherd the flock of God which is among you,**
> **serving as overseers, not by compulsion but willingly,**
> **not for dishonest gain but eagerly;**

nor as being lords over those entrusted to you, but being examples to the flock;

and when the Chief Shepherd appears, you will receive the crown of glory that does not fade away.

In this passage, the "elders" Peter is referring to are the pastors God had divinely called to shepherd the flock of God under the direction of the Chief Shepherd, Jesus. Peter uses the word *presbuteros*.[6] This word can be used to indicate an older person. But in this case, Peter describes himself as a *sumpresbuteros* or "fellow elder,"[7] indicating that he shares a likeness or equality in some way with the elders he is addressing. *Vine's* also indicates that for a person to be called an elder in this sense, he must have fulfilled the divine qualifications listed in Titus 1:6-9 and First Timothy 3:1-7.

Verses 5-6 go on to address the sheep:

Likewise you younger people, submit yourselves to your elders. Yes, all of you be submissive to one another, and be clothed with humility, for "God resists the proud, but gives grace to the humble."

Therefore humble yourselves under the mighty hand of God, that He may exalt you in due time.

This passage outlines the responsibilities of both pastor and congregation within the local church. As the pastor leads by loving example (which includes teaching the Word, correction, and even rebuke if necessary) and believers submit to him in humble obedience, the plan of God for that church can be fulfilled.

---

[6] Ibid., p. 20-21.
[7] Ibid., p. 21.

Satan Is Still Striking the Head

But that ideal situation is exactly what Satan is out to prevent. The enemy's purpose is to disrupt the spread of God's Kingdom, and his current strategy is the same as it has always been: *"...I will strike the Shepherd, and the sheep of the flock will be scattered"* (Matt. 26:31). If the enemy can succeed in his strategy to malign, discredit, and slander the pastor, the sheep of that particular flock will be scattered and wounded.

When people come against their pastor, Satan achieves a multi-level victory. The local congregation will be focused inward, unable to spread the Gospel as God has called them to do. When non-Christians witness the constant infighting and see the way the church destroys their leaders, they'll want no part of it. New converts who have just entered the church may be exposed to conflicts they can't handle. In the end, they may decide that Jesus is okay, but not church.

How do we stop being pawns in the hand of the enemy? How do we function as Jesus intended? First, we must recognize that the Kingdom of God is God's way of doing things. As I said earlier, God's Kingdom isn't like this world. It has different rules, different standards of judgment, and a different authority structure. It doesn't operate the way the world system does.

Second, we must examine ourselves for any sin we may have committed against our pastor, such as gossiping about him, harboring unforgiveness in our hearts toward him, or having rebellious attitudes about his way of leading the church. Should the Holy Spirit convict us of any wrongdoing in this area, we need to repent before God and allow Him to *change our ways*.

Adolescent Christians

Self-examination requires the ability to locate where we are in our walk with the Lord. You see, there are stages of spiritual development that a believer must go through in order to grow from a baby Christian to a mature adult Christian. Given this fact, at what stage are Christians most likely to resist limits imposed from a higher authority? At what stage do many believers think they know it all?

The baby stage of spiritual development is usually not the problem. For the most part, baby Christians love and appreciate their pastors. They are eager to grow in their knowledge of the Bible and in their relationship with God.

The problem arises when Christians reach "adolescence" in the spiritual walk and erroneously arrive at the conclusion that they have reached maturity. At that point, they often begin to pull away from their spiritual authority, thinking they don't need their pastor's guidance and help as much as they used to.

In the natural realm, adolescents are often egocentric and rebellious. They have attained a level of maturity but still have a lot to learn. Similarly, adolescent Christians often start mixing Bible teaching and worldly belief systems, which leads toward rebellion against their pastor's authority. They refuse to submit and make needed changes. They also refuse to recognize where they might be thinking wrong according to worldly "paradigms." They are in danger of never growing spiritually beyond adolescence.

Replacing Worldly Paradigms

A *paradigm* is an example of how things should be done, a framework into which we fit information. It is "given information" — facts that are so much a part of our lives, we often don't even recognize that these facts are in operation. For example, the sun rising each day is a paradigm. We don't even think about it. We take it for granted.

Besides the paradigms of the natural world, our daily lives are also filled with negative paradigms of this worldly system that adversely affect our attitudes and behaviors. These paradigms have to be replaced with the truth of God's Word. As we renew our minds daily with the Word, the worldly paradigms that have governed our lives in the past are replaced with Kingdom paradigms. This is the way we obey God's command to "be not conformed to this world."

Humanism and Democracy

For example, many destructive and deceptive paradigms come from humanism. These humanistic paradigms are in direct conflict with the Bible and permeate all aspects of our culture, including our public schools. Even democracy has its roots in humanism. When democracy honors the God of the Bible, it works. Democracy without God is dangerous.

Humanism is a movement that had its beginnings in the Renaissance. It began by examining Greek and Roman classics for their own sake rather than for their relevance to Christianity. According to George E. Duckworth in the *Microsoft Encarta Encyclopedia,* "a basic premise of humanism is that people are rational beings who possess within themselves the capacity for truth and goodness."[8]

Humanism promoted the idea that man could only reach his full potential if he examined the physical world and the perception of the senses apart from God. A Greek philosopher named Protagoras was popular in humanist circles and typified some

---

[8] George E. Duckworth, "Protagoras," *Microsoft Encarta Encyclopedia 99* (Mountain View, California: Microsoft Corporation, 1993-1998), p. 1.

of the tenants of humanistic thought. Of Protagoras, Duckworth notes, "The basis of his speculation was the doctrine that nothing is absolutely good or bad, true or false, and that each individual is therefore his or her own final authority; this belief is summed up in his saying: 'Man is the measure of all things.'"[9]

But in reality, *God* is the measure of all things. We are His creation, and we cannot reach our full potential without Him.

Humanism exalts the creation above the Creator. In fact, when joined to evolution, humanism invalidates even the idea of a creator.

When Charles Darwin developed his theory of evolution, his goal was to replace creationism, or the idea of a separate creation caused by God. Ronald L. Numbers of the *Microsoft Encarta Encyclopedia* states that Darwin "ruled out any role for God in the origin and development of living things."[10]

The theory of evolution presupposes that all aspects of life are evolving, including religion, government, etc. Regarding his theory of natural selection, Darwin stated that the individuals who most readily adapt to new situations are the ones who will survive.

Humanism teaches that an individual's actions should be based on what is best for him at the time. Thus, when humanistic thought is combined with the theory of evolution, the following implied conclusion is the result: Those who find adaptations for new situations will survive; those who will not adapt *won't* survive. Since God's truth is unchanging, the individuals who adhere to His truth are not important to society. They will not change and so are destined not to survive.

---

[9] Ibid.

[10] Ronald L. Numbers, "Creationism," *Microsoft Encarta Encyclopedia 99* (Mountain View, California: Microsoft Corporation, 1993-1998), p. 1.

Another dangerous deception exists in the marriage of humanism and evolution. In humanism, man seems to be given the place of central importance. But in the theory of evolution, man is merely a part of creation. Evolution is still in progress. Life forms and cultures are continually evolving.

The logical conclusion when these two worldly belief systems are combined is chilling. If man is merely one part of a larger creation, he is no more valuable than the rest of creation. And whereas man as a species is important (although, according to evolutionists, no more important than any other species, whether whales, kangaroo rats, or cockroaches), man as an individual is not.

The governmental form of humanism is democracy. Man is assumed to be the center of all things; therefore, man should be the authority on how to govern society. Since society is always evolving and changing, laws and culture must adapt to the times. Acceptable behavior becomes relative to the moment. Truth is the truth of the moment. Individuals are not as important as the whole. The good of the whole outweighs the rights of the individual.

Democracy is the best form of government a godless society could create. In a democracy, all people are represented. Life is equitable for most of the citizens most of the time. The goal of government is to maintain order and avoid anarchy.

Democracy requires the consent and cooperation of the governed. If the people are happy, the government survives. If the people are unhappy, changes are made through elections.

How Does God Govern His Kingdom?

But the Kingdom of God is a theocracy, not a democracy. No one elected Jesus Savior. There was no nominating process. Almighty God Himself proclaimed Him King of kings and Lord of lords.

In God's Kingdom, He makes the rules. There is no voting, no opinion polls, and no recall. Position and promotion in the Kingdom of God come only through divine appointment. The Bible says Jesus "appointed" or hand-picked His disciples (Luke 10:1).

God's Word is truth. It doesn't change with the times. The Ten Commandments are as valid today as when Moses received them. The Word of God lasts forever. Jesus said, *"Heaven and earth will pass away, but My words will not pass away"* (Mark 13:31).

The Early Church selected deacons to conduct the business of feeding widows and waiting tables (Acts 6:1-6); then Peter approved their selections. These deacons were appointed to serve, not to rule over the apostles in charge. The apostles were to devote themselves to study and prayer and to lead the church as Jesus led them.

In the same way, deacon and elder boards are not to rule over the pastor. Deacons and elders are to help lighten the pastor's load by serving in various aspects of ministry within the local church. But they are not to vote on the plans God has given to the pastor.

Members of a pastor's flock are to follow *him*. Sheep are not qualified to be shepherds. Church members are not appointed to be pastors; they are called to *follow* their pastors. They shouldn't vote on his instructions or plans either.

That's why church boards should be made up of other pastors or overseers who understand the workings of a local church. This makes much more sense than appointing businessmen or other lay workers to the board who have never had any experience in pastoring a church.

The World's Way:
Controlling Through Finances

Too often church boards try to run the church by controlling the pastor. One way this is accomplished is by controlling a pastor's salary. I once read in a ministry magazine about a study conducted to determine why pastors leave churches. According to the study, the major reason pastors leave their pastorates is an inadequate salary.

Pastors' families often live below the level of their congregations. To make ends meet, pastors often have to work a second job, or their wives work outside their homes. I know of one church that set the pastor's overall cost to the church below $50,000 per year — an amount well below the median income for that city. But a congregation who keeps their pastoral gift in a perpetual state of barely making ends meet is not giving honor to the gift or to the Giver.

This type of situation results in pastors trying to please the board rather than focusing on serving God. Happy board members give better raises. In the end, many churches get what they pay for.

The most amazing situation often takes place in churches. A pastor and his wife are led to a particular location to pioneer a church. They start out with no money and no people. But after years of hard work, they succeed in establishing a strong local church. Then after the church reaches a certain size, the pastor appoints a financial committee. Suddenly he is no longer in charge of the church. The financial committee is making all the decisions.

Kingdom Economics

The Bible has some interesting things to say about a pastor's salary. Paul said in First Timothy 5:17: *"Let the elders who rule well be counted worthy of double honor, especially those who labor in the word and doctrine."*

Vine's states that the term "double honor" could indicate an honorarium.[11] But are pastors who do a good job worthy of double salary? Verse 18 finishes the thought: *"For the Scripture says, 'You shall not muzzle an ox while it treads out the grain,' and, 'The laborer is worthy of his wages.'"* In context, the subject is money. As "elders who rule well," pastors are worthy of double salary.

What a radical idea! Decide on a fair salary, based on the median income of that geographic area. Then pay the pastor double that amount.

Next Sunday morning, take a long look at the man who stands behind the pulpit, preaching the Word from his heart. The Bible says he is worthy of double honor. God values that gift to His local body of believers so much, He wants him to be paid double wages!

There are other scriptures that address the money issue. The verses are talking about giving money. In Philippians 4:14-15

---

[11] W. E. Vine, M.A., *An Expository Dictionary of New Testament Words*, Vol. 2, p. 230.

(*KJV*), Paul uses the term "communicate" as he clearly talks about giving money. He makes the point that the Philippian church was the only church financially supporting him.

Notwithstanding ye have well done, that ye did communicate with my affliction.

Now ye Philippians know also, that in the beginning of the gospel, when I departed from Macedonia, no church communicated with me as concerning giving and receiving, but ye only.

Then in Galatians 6:6 (*KJV*), Paul says, *"Let him that is taught in the word communicate unto him that teacheth in all good things."* The *New King James Version* says it more clearly: *"Let him who is taught the word share in all good things with him who teaches."* The *Amplified Version* clarifies the verse even further: *"Let him who receives instruction in the Word [of God] share all good things with his teacher [contributing to his support]."*

The world wants workers for as little as possible, but Kingdom economics is different. Supply and demand is not an economic principle of God's Kingdom, but abundance for every good work is (2 Cor. 9:8). Third John 2 says, *"Beloved, I pray that you may prosper in ALL things and be in health, just as your soul prospers."*

The world economy is based on shortage. If someone is rich, then someone else has to be poor. But God gives all His people who walk in obedience to Him the power to get wealth (Deut. 8:18).

Our power to get wealth doesn't necessitate our taking it from someone else. In God, there is always more than enough.

In Malachi 3:10, God tells us to *prove* His faithfulness to bless us as we obey Him with our finances. We are to follow God's financial plan and see if He won't come through.

God is not stingy. Therefore, Christians who have Christ formed in them should not be stingy either.

Humanism:
From God-Centered to 'Me-Centered'

The humanistic world view is "me-centered"; the Bible is God-centered. Most Christians would accept the truth of that difference. However, they often balk when confronted with the truth about how extensively humanism has infiltrated their lives.

Believers often don't realize just how greatly humanism has distorted important relationships in their lives. For instance, the believer's relationships to the pastor and his local church are both vital to his spiritual growth and well-being. However, his own humanistic, selfish attitudes often corrupt these relationships and cause him to miss out on the fullness of God's blessings in his life.

We often use common phrases in our everyday speech that reveal this "me-centered" mindset. For example, most of us have heard or said such things as:

- "Well, you have to do what's best for you."

- "You deserve it."

- "You have to put your own needs first."

These are not expressions that fit within the Kingdom of God. Jesus gave us the opposite perspective:

- "Seek first the Kingdom of God" (Matt. 6:33).

- "Not what I will, but what You will be done" (Mark 14:36).

- "Your will be done on earth as it is in Heaven" (Matt. 6:10).

The "me-centered" view of humanism has changed the character of our society. It has made integrity and faithfulness almost obsolete concepts to the modern mind. This self-centered view makes man the center of the universe. The needs, wants, and desires of the individual person come first.

Here is an example of the modern "me-centered" problem. Several years ago, the church we were attending was meeting in a school for Sunday morning services. The church was in need of more workers for transportation and set-up. The pastor called a leadership meeting for the purpose of discussing the problem and finding a solution.

At the meeting, one of the leaders — a very vocal man — began to express his views. This man considered himself a very committed Christian, totally sold out to God. He said we would have to find more workers; until then, we would have to do whatever was needed. He spoke at some length on commitment and loyalty.

Then the pastor asked this man to help recruit more workers the next Sunday. The man said he would be glad to, but he wasn't going to be there. He would be gone for several Sundays. He and his wife had other plans.

The paradigm was in the man: "I will do what I can if I'm not busy doing something else." The Kingdom of God wasn't a priority to him; it was just another activity. He never considered changing his plans.

Would you change your plans if your pastor needed you?

That particular church held only one service per week. There was also one leadership meeting scheduled per month. But when the pastor announced that he wanted to start a Saturday evening outreach meeting, half the leaders complained that we were already overcommitted. These leaders eventually left the church. The pastor felt strongly that this was what God wanted next for our church, but they left anyway.

The Kingdom of God should be first in our lives. It is not just another activity. Matthew 6:33 (*AMP*) says, *"But seek (aim at and strive after) first of all His kingdom and His righteousness (His way of doing and being right), and then all these things taken together will be given you besides."*

Integrity involves honesty — the ability to answer questions with a straightforward "yes" or "no" without playing word games. A person of integrity takes responsibility for his or her own actions.

Sometimes people won't even admit responsibility for actions that don't constitute sin. They just don't want to be found in the wrong. For example, once when working with another leader on a mailing, I made a major mistake. The other leader checked my work, but we both missed the mistake. Later when the mistake was discovered, the leader's reaction was to ignore it. "Don't tell Pastor. He doesn't need to know. It will be okay." I knew I needed to take responsibility for the mistake, but I said nothing.

Pastor did find out, and he wasn't happy. The other leader criticized him for overreacting and minimized the original mistake. But by receiving my pastor's correction, I learned my lesson.

I have made other mistakes. Every time I do, I go to the pastor, tell him what I've done, and apologize. He isn't happy about the mistakes, but he does forgive me. He never holds my mistakes against me.

To a large extent, modern man has removed personal responsibility from society. This has caused an interesting side effect. People are supposedly no longer responsible for their actions; thus, how can they be accused of sinning? And if there is no sin, who needs forgiveness?

Without accepting responsibility for our actions, we cannot acknowledge our sin, nor can we ask for forgiveness. We become perpetual victims, always looking for a way to say, "It's not my fault." We try shifting the blame to others. "Yes" and "no" answers become "not exactly" as we endeavor to worm our way out of taking responsibility. We take offense if anyone tries to hold us accountable — *especially* our pastor.

Our culture would have us believe that the concept of sin is a myth. But if that were true, why did Jesus have to die? No, we have to acknowledge that we are sinners and ask God for forgiveness. Only then can we make Jesus the Lord of our lives.

Take this reasoning one step further. Can we ever escape from the self-destructive behaviors of sin? No, not without taking responsibility for our actions. The truth is, no one can *make* us do anything. We always have a choice. In Deuteronomy 30:19 (*KJV*), God said, *"I call heaven and earth to record this day against you, that I have set before you life and death, blessing and cursing: therefore CHOOSE LIFE, that both thou and thy seed may live."*

If we want to serve God and live free of sin, we have to understand that honesty, integrity, and taking personal responsibility for our actions are not optional qualities; they are *required.*

Matthew 21:23-27 provides a New Testament example of people denying responsibility. When the Jewish leaders asked Jesus a question, He answered with a question of His own, asking them where they thought John was from. The Jewish leaders never considered the real question. Their only interest was in how they would look to the people. They knew if they answered one way, the people would hate them for coming against John. If they answered the other way, they'd be in trouble with other leaders for appearing to follow John.

So the leaders lied, telling Jesus they didn't know. They didn't care about the truth — they cared only about how they looked to others.

In America, how people look to others is often more important to them than the truth. Unfortunately, the same situation also occurs in the Church.

But without the truth of God, we cannot be free: *"...If you abide in My word, you are My disciples indeed. And you shall know the truth, and THE TRUTH SHALL MAKE YOU FREE"* (John 8:31-32).

There is freedom in taking responsibility — freedom from nagging guilt; freedom to repent and move on. We expend so much unnecessary energy trying to get rid of guilt, but it's really very easy. We just need to say from our hearts, "I did it and I am sorry. I will never do it again." At that moment, guilt leaves and freedom comes.

A person of integrity can be trusted, whereas an unfaithful person who lacks integrity or refuses to take responsibility for his actions cannot be trusted. You see, faithfulness involves keeping one's word. In Psalm 15:1, David asks, *"Lord, who may abide in Your tabernacle? Who may dwell in Your holy hill?"* Then David lists the requirements, one of which is stated in verse 4: *"...he who swears to his own hurt and does not change."*

Keeping our word is a requirement for abiding with God. In everyday life, that means showing up to help if we said we would. It means arriving at our commitments on time. It means respecting authority and taking direction. It means doing the right thing when no one is watching.

Recently the leader of a national ministry commented on faithfulness. He explained that when he and his staff members travel to minister, they recruit volunteers from their partners in that locality. These volunteers man the book tables and help with other jobs as well. But increasingly, this ministry has had to recruit more workers than they need because many volunteers never show up. That's a demonstration of unfaithfulness.

Humanism has robbed our culture of three very important values that used to be part of our culture.

- First, we have lost the concept of absolute truth and embraced the belief that truth is relative.

- Second, we have lost the concept of personal responsibility, replacing it with blameshifting and protests of "It's not my fault." Consequences are no longer tied to behavior.

- Third, we no longer routinely lay down our lives for others. We are no longer our brother's keeper. We will help — but only if it's convenient and we have the time.

Obedience vs.
Disrespect for Authority

Not only has this "me-centered" mentality permeated our society today, but there is also a critical spirit operating in our country. Turn on any news channel, and you can watch it in operation. The news broadcasts are filled with people's adverse reactions and experts' negative opinions regarding political scandals and crises. Late-night talk shows add tasteless humor to the stories. The result is an atmosphere of total disrespect for authority. First Timothy 2:2 commands us to pray for those in authority, but it's so much easier to criticize and belittle them.

Unfortunately, this same critical spirit has crept into the Church. Have you ever asked someone, "What did you think of the sermon?" I have. But it's the wrong question to ask. What we think isn't important. But does it line up with the Word of God? Does it impact our lives? Those two questions *are* important.

We may go away from the pastor's sermon with an uncomfortable feeling that is more than likely the conviction of the Holy Spirit. But instead of responding to the message by changing, we often criticize the messenger. That kind of criticism undermines both our respect for authority and our ability to be obedient.

The Bible is our absolute standard of truth. If something lines up with the Bible, it cannot be argued away and our opinions about it become unimportant. Remember Deuteronomy 30:19: We are to *choose life*.

Obedience is a word that has become increasingly irrelevant in our culture. People use the word to explain how to train animals. But instead of teaching their children to be obedient, they focus on teaching them how to make choices.

However, sometimes the only choice is to obey or disobey. Obedience is very important to God. Disobedience is rebellion and has two roots: *disrespect for authority* and *pride*.

In First Samuel 15:23 (*AMP*), God spoke through Samuel to King Saul, giving the full meaning of disobedience: *"For rebellion is as the sin of witchcraft, and stubbornness is as idolatry and teraphim (household good luck images)...."* Then Samuel told Saul how God would handle his disobedience: *"...Because you have rejected the word of the Lord, He also has rejected you from being king."*

This scripture gives us God's opinion of disobedience. God is in charge of the universe, so His opinion is the only one that matters.

Isaiah 1:19 states, *"If you are willing and obedient, you shall eat the good of the land."* Jesus also indicates the value of obedience in Mark 3:35: *"For whoever does the will of God is My brother and My sister and mother."*

Obedience is not always pleasant. Hebrews 5:8 and 9 shows us the serious nature of obedience: *"Though He was a Son, yet He learned obedience by the things which He suffered. And having been perfected, He became the author of eternal salvation to all who obey Him."* First Samuel 15:22 states, *"Behold, to obey is better than sacrifice...."*

The Greek word for "obey" here is *hupokoe,* which means *to submit.*[12] The truth is, submission isn't true submission until it involves doing something we don't want to do.

But we are always being obedient to something. We are either obedient to our flesh and pride, or we are obedient to God. Obedience to our flesh and to pride leads to death. Obedience to God leads to life and righteousness.

We may think, *Well, I can understand the need to be obedient to God, but to the pastor too? He's only a man.* The pastor's ideas may not always seem as good as ours do. He may want to do something new, and we may want to do it "the same way we've always done it before."

But the pastor is our spiritual gift. He is to mature us and help the character of Jesus to be formed in us. God has supernaturally equipped him for the task. Our pastor will show us how to be conformed to the image of Jesus. Therefore, obedience to our pastor (unless his request is illegal, immoral, or unscriptural) is synonymous to obedience to the Lord — and obedience is not optional in God's Kingdom.

God will not bless disobedience, for He views it as rebellion, and He won't pour out His power on rebellious believers. What most believers don't understand, however, is that rebellion against their pastor is rebellion against God.

Pastors take it so personally when people will not follow them. But they take it personally because it *is* personal. The pastor knows that the church member who rejects him is really rejecting God.

---

[12] W. E. Vine, M.A., *An Expository Dictionary of New Testament Words*, Vol. 3 (Old Tappan, New Jersey: Fleming H. Revell Co., 1966), p. 20-21.

How can we be obedient to God whom we *can't* see if we can't be obedient to a pastor whom we *can* see?

Hebrews 13:17 couldn't make any clearer God's command to obey our pastors: *"Obey those who rule over you, and be submissive, for they watch out for your souls, as those who must give account. Let them do so with joy and not with grief, for that would be unprofitable for you."*

When we are in rebellion, we cannot profit from supernatural pastoring. Thus, we hinder the process of Jesus being formed in us.

Rooting Out the Sin of Pride

Check into the life of someone who rebels against his God-given authority, and you'll invariably discover that the person has a problem with pride. Pride was the first sin ever committed; therefore, all sin stems from pride. The root of the "me-centered" world-view is also pure pride. Pride says:

- "What I want is most important."

- "My comfort level is important."

- "I'm not doing anything I'm not comfortable doing."

- "My opinion needs to be considered at all times."

- "I don't need a pastor telling me what to do."

- "If I disagree with the pastor, I'm right."

- "I can hear from God. I don't miss it."

- "Pastor missed it that time."

- "Television ministries are as beneficial as going to church. I can get that corporate anointing in my living room."

- "Some people need three services a week. I don't."

Pride causes church splits. Pride destroys pastors and families. Pride renders a person unteachable. Pride opens the door to deception. Pride separates us from God.

Look at what God says about pride:

Pride goes before destruction, and a haughty spirit before a fall.

Proverbs 16:18

But He gives more grace. Therefore He says: "God resists the proud, but gives grace to the humble."

James 4:6

Therefore humble yourselves under the mighty hand of God, that He may exalt you in due time.

1 Peter 5:6

Pride says that our self-esteem is of major importance. However, the concept of self-esteem is not in the Bible. There is no way to establish our self-worth outside of God.

Humanism presents an interesting illusion when it says man is the center of the universe. On the other hand, a belief system that combines humanism and evolution places importance on creation as a whole. According to this paradigm, every creature is of equal importance. However, it does not build one's self-esteem to claim equality with an earthworm!

The issue of abortion further confuses the myth of self-esteem. Children are taught that a baby is not really a person until he or she is born. On the other hand, whales are whales whether in or out of the womb. We have to save the whales. It is very wrong to kill whales. But it is all right to kill babies before they are born.

This world-view may admit that each person has something unique and wonderful to contribute to this world. Nevertheless, a woman has the right to kill the life growing inside her womb because the baby is not a person until it is born. Therefore, the baby is not as important as the mother's right to choose.

Psalm 139:13-16 explains God's view of the unborn:

For You formed my inward parts; You covered me in my mother's womb.

I will praise You, for I am fearfully and wonderfully made; marvelous are Your works, and that my soul knows very well.

My frame was not hidden from You, when I was made in secret, and skillfully wrought in the lowest parts of the earth.

Your eyes saw my substance, being yet unformed. And in Your book they all were written, the days fashioned for me, when as yet there were none of them.

God created us all. He fashioned every one of our days on this earth before we were ever born.

Therefore, abortion advocates are wrong when they claim that a baby is not a person until he or she is born. No child is an accident to God. Each person is important.

Romans 12:3 has a sobering view of our self-worth: *"For I say, through the grace given to me, to everyone who is among you, not to think of himself more highly than he ought to think, but to think soberly, as God has dealt to each one a measure of faith."*

Our value is totally dependent on God. Jesus gave His life for each of us. We are beyond price, for we cost God all He had. In light of this truth, what pride can we hold on to? God did all the work, and our only value comes from Him.

Even our natural talents and abilities are nothing to God. He doesn't promote us according to our educational credentials or talents, but according to our willingness, obedience, and faithfulness. He often asks us to do things we cannot do in the natural so that when the task is finished, the glory is all His.

Our Own Righteousness: 'As Filthy Rags'

It's so easy to take pride in our accomplishments. We become proud of what we do for God and often judge those who don't do as much as we do. In our pride, we try to create our own righteousness by our works. But only the redemptive work of Jesus produces true righteousness in God's sight. Righteousness based on our own works is as filthy rags to Him (Isa. 64:6).

I learned what God meant by "filthy rags" when I began to work as a nurse. When I first started my nursing career, hospitals were different. Instead of being sent to nursing homes, people with terminal cancer often died in hospitals after being admitted as "terminal care" patients. As the cancer ate away the bodies of these unfortunate patients, they developed wounds that wouldn't heal. Decaying flesh and massive infections within these wounds caused large amounts of drainage that emitted very strong odors.

I was one of the nurses in this ward. Every shift we would change the dressings and clean the patients. Sometimes we did it more often. It could take an hour or more to clean one person. The drainage would seep through the dressings and the patient's gown and get all over the bed linens.

When I'd enter the room, the stench from the drainage would be nauseating. But I'd smile and talk to the patient as I took off the soiled, foul-smelling dressings. I'd clean the wounds and cover them with clean dressings. Then I had to bathe the patient and clothe him or her in a clean gown. Finally, I would make the bed.

For a few minutes, the stench would disappear and the patient would feel refreshed and clean. But when I checked the patient one last time before leaving the room, I'd see a spot of drainage about the size of a dime already seeping through the clean dressing.

The righteousness we try to create through our own works is like those filthy, foul-smelling dressings on those cancer patients. Apart from God, the best we can do *stinks*.

Above all, pride stinks. It will always seep through the most attractive façade we might try to hide behind. Therefore, we have to reject our own righteousness and accept God's righteousness through Christ Jesus. This takes a daily, conscious decision on our part.

As we die to ourselves and accept God's righteousness, Jesus is formed in us. We come to a place in our spiritual walk where we have nothing left of ourselves to take pride in. This is when God can truly use us to His glory.

God makes a point of regularly exposing our pride so we can root it out. To do this, He often uses our pastor. However, too often we resist our pastor's correction. We'd rather keep the pride and reject the pastor!

When we resist God's work in us, we make Him resist us. But when we yield to Him and willingly become His bondservants, He exalts us.

Servants of the Most High God

The concept of servanthood produces an immediate negative reaction in many of us. For instance, even though we may love the story of Joseph, the part we like is the end of the story, where Joseph rises out of slavery to become a leader with power and authority over all of Egypt.

Yet the truth is, Joseph was never actually freed. He remained a slave under the ultimate authority of Pharaoh. After Joseph's death, a new king arose in Egypt who didn't know Joseph (Exod. 1:8). This new Pharaoh decided to deal harshly with the children of Israel by enslaving them. (I wonder if he remembered that Joseph was never freed?)

But even though servants are not honored in our culture, that is exactly what we are in the Kingdom of God — bondservants of Jesus Christ. You see, Jesus paid for us (1 Cor. 6:20). He redeemed us with His blood from the kingdom of darkness (Col. 1:13-14). We are not our own anymore. We belong to Him.

Talented, educated people often have a difficult time serving in a local church because they think they have something special to offer God. Sometimes it seems like they think they did Jesus a favor by accepting Him! They want to lead instead of submitting to their pastor's leadership as God intended. But God isn't impressed with their natural talents and abilities. He is only impressed with obedience, faithfulness, and humility.

I've run into people like this when I've tried to recruit workers for children's ministry. Gifted musicians feel called to use their "gift" to honor God, but they almost never want to join the children's worship team. Other people are sure they have a teaching gift, but they're also certain they are called to teach *adults*. When offered teaching positions in the children's ministry, they decline. Then there are those people who, amazingly, have to "pray" about whether or not they should help clean up after a church dinner!

Laying down your life for another sounds lofty and romantic. However, the glamour may fade when you're asked to change diapers in the church nursery. That doesn't sound as attractive, but it's the kind of service God is asking of you when He tells you to lay down your life.

In many churches, twenty percent of the people do eighty percent of the work. But Jesus was very specific about the importance of being a servant.

Jesus paid the price for our salvation. When we acknowledge Him as Lord, we become His servants, just as He was a servant. In Matthew 12:18, the Father said, *"Behold! My Servant whom I have chosen, my Beloved in whom My soul is well pleased!..."*

Even Jesus called Himself a Servant: *"Just as the Son of Man did not come to be served, but to serve, and to give His life a ransom for many"* (Matt. 20:28). On more than one occasion, He placed Himself in a servant's role and physically served His disciples (John 13:1-10).

The Bible describes the various aspects of our relationship with God. We are the children of God, joint heirs with Christ (Rom. 8:15-17). We are the righteousness of God in Christ (2 Cor. 5:21). But we are also servants of the Most High God (Eph. 6:6). In Mark 9:35, Jesus said that if we want to be first, we have to be last, the servants of all. He also commended good and faithful servants (Matt. 25:21). Jesus even told parables about unprofitable servants, saying they were not welcomed into the Kingdom (Matt. 25:30).

The writers of the New Testament knew they were servants. Peter, Jesus' brother James, Paul, and John all referred to themselves as bondservants. They willingly submitted to the will of Jesus, laying down their lives to serve Him and His Church.

The word for "deacon" means *servant* or *serving*.[13] More than ever, the Church needs a revelation of this concept of serving and servants. Christians are to humble themselves and serve others. A person can't lead if he can't follow. The Church desperately needs more servants.

A pastor I know started a Bible school designed for anyone who sensed a call to the ministry. This school offered students both classroom and practical training. One afternoon per week, the students sat in the church office. Their job was to talk to people. They were to answer the phone and counsel people as needed.

---

[13] W. E. Vine, M.A., *An Expository Dictionary of New Testament Words* (Old Tappan, New Jersey: Fleming H. Revell Co., 1966), pp. 272-273.

These students also took turns cleaning the church. They knew they were called to full-time ministry, but they cheerfully cleaned toilets, vacuumed the church carpets, and emptied the trash. They even cleaned up after weddings.

The willingness to be a servant is a requirement for Christian leadership. If we cannot serve others, we are not qualified to lead.

Pastors who require this type of commitment and service from their congregation are not usually very popular. Sometimes they are even accused of being abusive. But humility is a big part of spiritual maturity, and learning to serve is a big part of humility.

Let me emphasize again — when we serve and obey our pastor, we are serving and obeying God. Remember the Olympic athlete. The pastor is our spiritual "coach." He gets us into position to run our race (Heb. 12:1) and win our crown (2 Tim. 4:8).

It was a custom in Bible times for people to honor someone by giving him servants. For example, Pharaoh gave Abraham servants (Gen. 12:16). The servants had no choice; they had to go with Abraham. Servants served where they were sent.

Well, God gives us serving assignments as well, especially in the local church. So as we determine to accept the pastor God has given us, we must also be prepared to serve him — and that includes obeying him.

In Luke 17:10, Jesus said, *"So likewise you, when you have done all those things which you are commanded, say, 'We are unprofitable servants. We have done what was our duty to do.'"* True servants of God look for opportunities to serve. They serve with joy. They are excited about being able to serve. They love the one they serve. They are available to him. They follow his instructions.

A Church Is Not a Business

Many people don't receive their gift of a pastor because they make the mistake of comparing a church to a business and their pastor to a supervisor or a Chief Executive Officer. However, the Kingdom of God is *not* a business. Business management techniques and theories do not fit into a church.

I have been a registered nurse for twenty-five years. I worked in hospitals and nursing homes for fifteen years; later, I worked three years for an insurance company. I have seen how businesses handle employees. I even took a college course in supervision. I can say from firsthand experience that the comparison between a church and a business doesn't hold up under scrutiny.

Important inconsistencies are apparent when comparing management practices and the Bible. First, management theories change over time. I personally suffered through several management theories while I was working.

For example, one theory I encountered was as follows: *With proper systems in place, individuals are not important. The systems will keep the business running.* Another theory was that managers are a type of servants to the workers because they supply the workers with what they need to do their jobs.

The world's management theories come and go, but the management system of God's Kingdom is simple and eternal. God is permanently in charge. Jesus is King of the Kingdom. He makes the rules, sets the standards, and pays the wages.

There are no unions or grievance procedures, and the one policy-and-procedure manual — the Bible — is never revised.

Supervision of the workers is handled by the ministry gifts, who are appointed by Jesus and anointed by the Holy Spirit to lead. That anointing flows from the Head, Jesus, down to each individual ministry gift.

In God's Kingdom, departments are called churches; department heads are called pastors; and workers are called servants, children of God, joint heirs, and the righteousness of God in Christ.

Promotion in the Kingdom is by appointment only, and job requirements are not position specific. Instead, the qualities of willingness, faithfulness, obedience, loyalty, and the ability to walk in love are the primary requirements for positions. Humility is required of leaders — specific knowledge of the job is not.

You see, God is God. You can do anything He assigns you to do.

Another important, distinctive difference between a business and the Kingdom of God is that disgruntled employees are handled very differently. In business, if workers become unhappy with the supervisor, the supervisor can just be replaced. For instance, at times the nurses I worked with would get disgruntled. The next thing I knew, there would be a change in head nurses.

But God doesn't abandon the leaders He has called and appointed. For example, when Miriam and Aaron complained against Moses, God became angry with them, and Miriam contracted leprosy (Num. 12:1-10).

Numbers 14 then gives the account of the people's rebellion against their leaders. The people complained against Moses and Aaron (Num. 14:2). The congregation wanted to select another leader and return to Egypt (v. 4). They even wanted to stone Moses and Aaron (v. 10).

What was God's response? He wanted to kill all the children of Israel and start over with a new group for Moses to lead. When the workers complained against the leader, God wanted to replace the workers! In the end, that rebellious generation died in the desert.

The rebels didn't make it into the Promised Land because God held them responsible for how they followed Moses. When the people rebelled against Moses, God considered it rebellion against Himself. God takes it personally when we rebel against His leaders.

God still expects us to honor our leaders, for there are still consequences for rebellion, disloyalty, and disobedience. Those consequences may not catch up to us immediately, but unless there is repentance, there will be a judgment.

God also holds leaders accountable for *their* disobedience. Moses didn't make it into the Promised Land either. God didn't allow him to enter the land because he had sinned in anger at the waters of Meribah (Num. 27:12-14). No matter who the transgressor is, God never honors rebellion.

Most business managers try to keep the workers happy and appreciated because they know their jobs are on the line. God's leaders, on the other hand, are not to be men-pleasers. They are required to walk in the God-kind of love found in First Corinthians 13, but their job is to lead the people God assigns to them and bring them to maturity. Pastors are to follow God and lead their sheep.

Sometimes we complain that we aren't appreciated. But appreciated by whom? In God's Kingdom, we are not to work for the approval of men. We are to serve *God.*

Jesus died for me more than 1,900 years before I was born. He is preparing a place for me in Heaven. He loves me. He allows me to work in His Kingdom. He pays wages as I diligently seek Him (Heb. 11:6). I can walk in divine health and prosper (3 John 2). He trusts me with an assignment in His Kingdom. What more appreciation do I need?

Pastors and their wives feel great pressure to thank their workers. Church members expect this treatment. Yet sometimes believers are dissatisfied with the affirmation they receive.

I could never relate to that attitude. For instance, I once worked in the helps ministry of a church for ten years. During that time, I asked God how I could most effectively help in the church. He told me to support the pastor's wife.

So I made clothes for the pastor's family, babysat their children, occasionally stocked their refrigerator, and so on. I never received one thank-you note, but I never needed one. I was grateful that God would give me such a special assignment. I felt honored to serve the pastor's wife and family.

Pastors can get together at conferences and talk about running churches and handling people. That's their business. *Our* business is to grow up and serve God with joy. We should thank God that He has trusted us with an assignment in His Kingdom.

Walking in the Fear of God

There's another reason believers don't receive the pastoral gift Jesus has given them. Many times they lack a healthy fear of God.

The Church has emphasized the love of God at the expense of teaching believers to fear God. Psalm 111:10 says, *"The fear of the Lord is the beginning of wisdom...."*

Now look at Proverbs 1:7 (*AMP*): *"The reverent and worshipful fear of the Lord is the beginning and the principal and choice part of knowledge [its starting point and its essence]; but fools despise skillful and godly Wisdom, instruction, and discipline."*

Too often we react in rebellion when we hear a message we don't like. We decide the pastor spends too much time talking about money. We resist commitment to the local church. We even leave the church God assigns us. Instead of choosing to fear God, we decide to be wise in our own eyes.

Proverbs 3:7 warns about that kind of carnal reaction: *"Do not be wise in your own eyes; fear the Lord and depart from evil."* Psalm 55:19 puts it another way: *"...because they do not change, therefore they do not fear God."*

Our God is still a consuming fire. If the God of love is the only God you know, you need to expand your vision. Read the story of Sodom and Gomorrah. Read the Book of Revelation. God does not change. He still hates disobedience. Disobedience is still sin. Sin still brings consequences.

God is our Lord and Savior, our Friend, and our Dad. But He is also the Almighty God of the universe. He deserves and requires honor.

Notice that the fear of the Lord is the *beginning* of wisdom. The attaining of wisdom is a journey, and our pastors help lead us along the way. One way they do that is by pointing out areas in our lives that need correction. Our appropriate response to the conviction of the Holy Spirit or the correction of our pastor is to *change*. Only fools despise instruction (Prov. 1:7).

Psalm 128 is all about the fear of the Lord:

Blessed is every one who fears the Lord, who walks in His ways.

When you eat the labor of your hands, you shall be happy, and it shall be well with you.

Your wife shall be like a fruitful vine in the very heart of your house, your children like olive plants all around your table.

Behold, thus shall the man be blessed who fears the Lord.

The Lord bless you out of Zion, and may you see the good of Jerusalem all the days of your life.

Yes, may you see your children's children. Peace be upon Israel!

You see, there are benefits to fearing the Lord. God promises abundant blessings and a peaceful, fruitful life to those who fear God.

The Christian life is a life of balance, and the One who keeps everything in balance is the Holy Spirit. He doesn't want us to focus only on the fear of God. That's just as destructive as seeing only the love and mercy side of God. We are to walk in the fear of the Lord, but we are to also abide in His overwhelming love.

It's time for us to renounce humanism and pride and get the world out of the Church, just as the apostle Paul admonished us: *"This I say, therefore, and testify in the Lord, that you should no longer walk as the rest of the Gentiles walk, in the futility of their mind"* (Eph. 4:17). It's time to fear God and serve in His army. It's time to receive the gift of our pastor.

Chapter 4
Receiving Your Gift

Therefore He says: "When He ascended on high, He led captivity captive, and gave gifts to men."

— Ephesians 4:8

When we are born again, that's only the beginning. A regeneration process has been initiated, beginning with a new spirit born of His Spirit. After that, it is up to us to renew our minds with God's Word so the regeneration process can progress from the inside to our outward man. We can actually have the "mind of Christ" (1 Cor. 2:16).

Do Mature Christians Really Need a Pastor?

But is there ever a stage in that regeneration process where we cease to need a pastor? Do we ever reach a level of maturity that makes a pastor an unnecessary option?

First Corinthians 13 contains a sixteen-point test of maturity centered around walking in love. Read it and test yourself on how well you're doing. Then in John 13:34, Jesus commanded us to love one another. The Greek word for the kind of love Jesus was talking about is *agape*. That same word is used in First Corinthians 13. *Agape* is the God-kind of love.

In verse 35, Jesus goes on to say, *"By this all will know that you are My disciples, if you have love for one another."* Once again, the word for love in this scripture is *agape*. Then Ephesians 4:16 states that the entire Body of Christ is to be knit together, working effectively together to grow and to be built up in love. The Greek word for this love is again *agape*, the God-kind of love.

71

Are these scriptures on love a reality in your life? Do you show others the God-kind of love? Are you moved with compassion? Has anyone ever accused you of being a Christian? Has anyone ever asked you why your life is different? Has anyone ever asked how to receive what you have? Has your love ever failed? When was the last time it did?

Are you fully mature in God? Until you are, you need a pastor.

But even if we were perfect, we would still need a pastor. A pastor will bring us into unity with other saints, which is necessary if we are going to effectively win this world for Jesus.

You see, Jesus isn't coming back to appear on national television; He's coming back to collect those with whom *we* have shared the Gospel. No one person can do the job. God didn't design His Kingdom that way. We have to join together with other Christians in other churches and go win the world. And as new believers come into the Kingdom, we must assimilate them into a good local church and then go win some more souls for the Lord.

Jesus is coming back for His Church, not for a bunch of lone rangers. He isn't interested in folks going out to do their own thing.

The Kingdom of God is *God's* way of doing things — not ours. We are to be connected to a local church. But if we are going to fulfill God's purpose within our local church, we have to receive our gift. And to receive our gift, we have to recognize it.

Recognizing Your Gift

We are all drawn to prominent leaders in the church. We recognize apostles, prophets, and teachers. Maybe we were even saved through an evangelist. But how do we recognize our pastor?

The Holy Spirit will show you the pastor He has given to you. First Corinthians 2:12 says, *"Now we have received, not the spirit of the world, but the Spirit who is from God, that we might know the things that have been freely given to us by God."* Here are some practical signs to look for:

1. *Look for the pastor, not the church.* You may be tempted to judge pastors by their churches or their programs. Is there a youth program for the teens or a singles ministry? But without the pastor, there is no church. The pastor is the important part. Don't worry about the rest. When you find your pastor, the church will meet your needs.

2. *A true pastor will stand in the office of a pastor.* He will probably be in full-time ministry and be widely recognized as a pastor.

3. *A person only has one pastor at a time.* A close, godly friend is not your pastor. The person who got you born again is not your pastor. Your spiritual father or mother is not your pastor.

Although older, more mature Christians do have wisdom to offer, only God-appointed pastors are able to pastor supernaturally. God has given each of us a pastor, and His perfect will is that we receive and esteem that gift in love.

Look for that peace within, that "knowing that you know." Don't look at the circumstances. Don't look at the driving distance to the church. Don't look at the programs it offers. Look on the inside of you. If you sense a peace in your spirit, go for it.

When you find your pastor, make a note of it. Write down why you know this is the one. When the offenses come, get out that written account. Review it and be encouraged. Remind yourself that God does not change His mind.

Three Stages
Of Receiving Your Gift

People experience three stages when they make major changes in their lives, whether they get married, change jobs, or find a new church. These three stages certainly apply to receiving a new pastor.

The first stage is the romance stage. At first, everything the pastor says is wonderful. We love every message. We hang on to his every word.

Then the romance fades. We see the pastor mowing his lawn. We catch him yelling at his kids. Maybe the church has some imperfect folks in it. Or our children may start to complain that they don't like the youth group. Perhaps we hear a sermon that reveals an area in our lives needing correction.

During this stage, we can begin to wonder if we made a mistake in coming to that particular church. It's a dangerous time. If we're not careful, we may become disillusioned and step out of God's will.

At this stage, a lot of Christians lack the necessary staying power to remain committed to their church. They confuse happiness for joy and forget that following Jesus involves some work. They forget they have to die to themselves so Jesus can be formed in them. They forget that Jesus said in Mark 8:34, *"...Whoever desires to come after Me, let him deny himself, and take up his cross, and follow Me."* (In other words, "Find God's will and do it.")

It is at this stage that offense often comes to call, and too many Christians welcome him in. That's why so many Christians never make it to the third phase.

The third phase is realistic acceptance. In this phase, happiness is replaced with joy. We find our place in our local church. We accept the pastor as our gift. We make a conscious decision to follow him. We recognize the only criteria for not obeying our pastor: "Is this illegal, immoral, or unscriptural?"

This stage is the beginning of spiritual maturity. We receive, welcome, and truly accept the gift of our pastor. We value his supernatural pastoring, and, thus, we go on with God.

Because everyone goes through these three stages on the road to spiritual maturity, new believers would usually do well to stay in the church where they got saved. They received the salvation message through that particular pastor. There is probably more the Holy Spirit wants to say through him.

Make a Demand on the Anointing

After you find your pastor, expect supernatural things to happen. Your pastor is anointed to pastor supernaturally, so every time you go to church, go expecting. Look for a word or a touch from God for you personally.

· When I got saved in the '70s, most of us in the church attended every service. We used to say we wanted all God had for us. Today I still go to every church service. I know that God will speak through my pastor. I expect something every time. I have never been disappointed.

Over the years I've consistently placed a demand on the pastoral anointing, and it has caused amazing growth in my life. Problems that I struggled with for years have just dropped away. At least four major problems have been eliminated from my life since finding my current pastor. As Isaiah 10:27 (*KJV*) says, "*...the yoke shall be destroyed because of the anointing.*"

One area I struggled with for many years was depression. When I was in my late thirties, the depression reached a crisis point. At the time, my husband's parents had moved in with us, and we were experiencing problems with infertility. We had other areas of major stress in our lives as well. I found myself becoming angry and bitter inside. Each fall, I'd cycle into a major depression. I was often on medication for my condition, but only once did I gather the courage to go forward for prayer at church. For the most part, I just lived with it.

Then one day, I noticed the depression was gone. I have now been depression-free for years!

We have seen that Ephesians 4 lists several benefits God provides through the ministry gifts. Spiritual maturity is one of those benefits. But the goal of spiritual maturity is most effectively attained in the local church as we receive consistently from our pastor. When the pastoral anointing is in operation, supernatural pastoring takes place, and God is able to give us what we need. We receive from the Holy Spirit through our pastor.

Another benefit of receiving your pastor is protection from deception. Think of the three-strand cord that is not easily broken (Eccl. 4:12). One strand is the Word of God; the second strand is the Holy Spirit; and the third strand is the pastor.

Many Christians have fallen into error or deception — a pitfall that is completely avoidable with proper pastoral protection. This is how that protection works.

We should all read the Bible for ourselves. But as we read the Word, it is open to interpretation. We can become confused. We may listen for the Holy Spirit to enlighten us. But sometimes the situation is emotionally charged, making it difficult to be objective. These are the times we need a third, objective voice. Our pastor can help us discern the truth.

This system of protection works only as we are submitted to our pastor. We must stay humble, for we may have to admit we are wrong. In this way, supernatural pastoring helps us avoid error and know the truth. God uses our pastor to stabilize our lives and keep us from remaining as *"...children, tossed to and fro, and carried about with every wind of doctrine, by the sleight of men, and cunning craftiness, whereby they lie in wait to deceive"* (Eph. 4:14 *KJV*).

More Benefits of Receiving a Pastor

Matthew 10:41 (*AMP*) gives us another benefit of receiving our pastor: *"He who receives and welcomes and accepts a prophet because he is a prophet shall receive a prophet's reward...."* Jesus was speaking to people of the Old Covenant. Under that covenant, there was only one ministry gift — the prophet. Under the New Covenant, Jesus gave us five ministry gifts, including the pastor.

Therefore, this same principle applies to our relationship with our pastor. If we receive, welcome, and accept him as the pastor God has given us, we will receive a pastor's reward. The important words are *receive, welcome,* and *accept.* We are to receive our pastor. We are to welcome him into our lives as a gift. We are to accept what he says and make the changes he indicates are necessary.

Second Timothy 3:16-17 tells us the purpose of God's Word that is preached from the pulpits of local churches around the world:

> **All Scripture is given by inspiration of God, and is profitable for doctrine, for reproof, for correction, for instruction in righteousness,**
>
> **that the man of God may be complete, thoroughly equipped for every good work.**

We receive, welcome, and accept what our pastor teaches us from the Word — even when it's hard to hear — and we make the correction. Then we obtain our reward: more of Jesus' character is formed in us. The work of the pastor is to equip and mature. So when we receive, welcome, and accept his ministry in our lives, we are further equipped and brought to maturity.

As we receive our pastor, we also find help in fulfilling God's command to tell others about Jesus. God wants all men to hear the Gospel. He has a plan for reaching every geographic area, and He gives that plan to the pastors of local churches. As we help our pastor fulfill the vision God has given him, we do our part to reach the lost within our community and around the world.

Most of us learned to play "Follow the Leader" as children. The principle behind this childhood game becomes very significant in the Kingdom of God. The pastor is God's leader of the local church. The leader has the plan. We are to follow the leader — the pastor. The Church is to reach the whole world with the Gospel. When we follow our leaders, we reach the world. It really is that simple.

Believers without pastors and churches operate at a disadvantage. What do they do with the people they lead to the Lord? Do they send the baby Christians to church while they stay home?

Leading someone to the Lord isn't enough. We have a responsibility to help that new believer become rooted and growing in his spiritual walk. That means we have a responsibility to help him find a good pastor.

The Pastor as a Catalyst

The world operates according to a process called "networking." In this process, it isn't *what* you know but *whom* you know.

In the Kingdom of God, it works this way: Each local church contains a body of believers gathered around a head. The head is the pastor, who acts as a catalyst for many of God's purposes to be fulfilled within that local body.

A catalyst is a chemical that triggers a reaction without being a part of the reaction itself. Without the catalyst, there is no reaction.

For instance, a pastor may act as a catalyst to bring about a supernatural connection between two people. Two strangers may find themselves interacting because they both know the pastor. This can happen both within the church and between churches or ministries. Let me give you an example of how this works.

A construction worker who had recently moved to our area started coming to our church. Later his wife and children joined him. I had never met the man's family; I didn't even know what they looked like. But when one of their children was hospitalized, I sensed strongly that I should go visit to the hospital to visit the child.

While I was at the hospital, I met the mother, who later became a wonderful friend. We have remained friends for thirteen years. But we wouldn't have met without the catalyst of the church and the pastor.

Here's another example: My husband and I own a timeshare condominium. One year we were unable to use it, so we offered it to all our friends. No one was interested, since it is located several states away. Then the Holy Spirit led us to offer it to a couple in ministry who come yearly to speak in our church. We didn't know the couple personally.

This couple lived within driving distance of the condo, so they accepted our offer. They had been traveling in ministry for some time and needed a rest. But people in the ministry learn to be skeptical of folks offering gifts. It would have been difficult for the couple to accept our offer if we had not all known our pastor.

God joins people together around a pastor. Pastors know other ministry gifts, so God can use them to bring strangers together to accomplish His goals. God can also bring strangers together just to be a blessing. But it all begins with a pastor.

Without a pastor, believers are out on their own, and God is limited in how He can use them or bless them. Despite this fact, many still refuse to receive their pastor.

Several times I've had people complain to me that another person has helped them more than the pastor ever did. This type of comment is so short-sighted. These people don't recognize the simple truth: Without the pastor, they may never have known that special person. Pastors are catalysts. They make things happen.

Caring for Your Gift

What does it mean to care for the gift of your pastor? It's all about honor. You honor Jesus, the Head of the Church, when you honor the person He has ordained to stand in that ministry office.

On the road to Damascus, Jesus accused Saul of persecuting Him, even though Saul was actually persecuting Christians (Acts 9:5). And in Matthew 25:40 (*KJV*), Jesus said, *"...Verily I say unto you, Inasmuch as ye have done it unto one of the least of these my brethren, ye have done it unto me."*

So when we honor our pastor, we honor Jesus. If we dishonor our pastor, we dishonor Jesus.

Would you allow Jesus to wear worn-out clothes? Would you pick apart one of Jesus' sermons? Would you refuse Jesus a pay increase? Would you gossip behind His back? These questions are sobering but necessary to consider.

Honoring our pastor consists of several elements. We must pray for him and his family. We must respect him. We must see to his general well-being. We must encourage him to take adequate time for rest. We must be loyal to him and bless him. Let's look at these elements one at a time.

First, we must pray for our pastor. James 5:16 says, *"...The effective, fervent prayer of a righteous man avails much."* First Thessalonians 5:17-18 says to *"pray without ceasing, in everything give thanks...."*

The Bible also commands that we pray for those in authority that our days may be spent in peace (1 Tim. 2:1-2). Our pastors are included in that scripture, for they have spiritual authority over us. As shepherds, they lead, guide, and watch over us.

Most Christians do not pray daily for their pastors. At the most, they may pray weekly. But this is disobedient to the Word.

Is every aspect of your church or your own personal life peaceful? If the answer to that question is no, consider how often you pray for your pastor. Your lack of prayer may be part of the problem. So much strife in the church and at home would stop immediately if believers would just pray.

If you don't pray for your pastor regularly, simply repent and start praying. Pray in English. Pray in the Spirit. Pray a scriptural prayer from a book. But just pray! If the Holy Spirit shows you specific things to pray for, just keep the information to yourself and keep praying. Faithfully intercede for your gift; then look to Heaven for your peaceful reward.

Second, we are to respect our pastor. "Respect" means *to admire; to give consideration and attention to.*[14] Respect is due on two levels: 1) We are to respect the gift because of the Giver. In other words, we respect our pastor because we love and honor Jesus. 2) We are to respect the gift for the sake of the gift.

[14] Gordon Carruth, Eugene Ehrlich, Stuart Berg Flexner, Joyce M. Hawkins, *Oxford American Dictionary* (New York: Avon Books, 1980), p. 772.

We care for, admire, and give consideration and attention to our pastor because he means so much to our lives.

Showing honor and respect to our pastor requires being obedient to him. We are to obey any requests that are not immoral, illegal, or unscriptural. If there is anything wrong with the pastor's request, God will deal with him about it.

If we tell our child to come inside and he continues to play, that disobedience demonstrates disrespect. In the same way, if our pastor asks us to come to church on time and we always arrive late, we are showing disrespect to him. Or if our pastor asks for a salary increase and we say no, that is also demonstrating disrespect.

I know of a pastor who had built up some debt while the church went through a difficult time financially. The pastor had gone without a salary for several weeks, but the financial board refused to help him pay off that debt. They just asked to see his bills and offered to help him make a budget. The board's response to their pastor's need was disrespectful, arrogant, and rude — but it happened.

My first pastor had strong opinions about salaries. I remember his comments on the subject. He said pastors should be paid a salary that enables them to maintain the same standard of living as the rest of the community. Many churches won't support that perspective. Those churches don't deserve pastors. In dishonoring their pastor, they dishonor God.

Third, we must see to our pastor's general well-being. Most pastors are either overworked or in danger of overworking. Pastoring a church is a 24-hour-a-day job. Pastors often have to leave town in order to truly rest. Many wives are also called to work alongside their husbands. The entire family can become stressed by the pastor's busy schedule.

Therefore, a congregation should encourage their pastor to take vacations. They should send their pastor to a yearly pastors' conference. They should encourage him to take occasional short trips away from home with his family. Honoring one's pastor is recognizing his need for refreshing.

We should also look for ways to help decrease our pastor's workload. I've found that there are a lot of tasks around the church and the pastor's home we can do that don't require his attention. For example, we may be able to help him by washing his car or mowing his lawn. Every hour we can give and every task we can do for our pastor gives him more time to pray, study, or be with his family.

A word of caution here: Don't serve your pastor unless you are willing to be a servant as the Bible commands. A servant never elevates himself above the one he is serving. The big danger in serving a pastor when you don't have a servant's heart is that it opens you to the sin of inappropriate familiarity.

You see, if we are not truly servants, we may start out helping the pastor. But as we spend time working closely with our pastor, we begin to notice his faults. This can start a deceptive process. We start thinking we know more than the pastor and can do things better than he can. Familiarity then breeds contempt. Instead of honoring our gift, we begin to hold him in contempt. We become offended. We cannot receive from him anymore.

But servants love the ones they serve. Their goal is to see their pastor succeed, so they look for ways to serve him. Servants see faults, but they don't let those faults affect the way they value and esteem their gift. They find joy and are grateful for the opportunity to serve their pastor, knowing they are serving Jesus as well.

Servants also know how to keep their mouths shut. They can be trusted not to betray a confidence. Betrayal of a confidence can destroy a pastor and his family. Gossip can destroy churches. That's why true servants never disclose anything personal or private in nature that they may see or hear.

As you serve your pastor, don't hold high expectations for thank-you notes and gestures of appreciation from him. Remember whom you are really serving and honoring — Jesus. Whatever you do for any other Christian, you do for Him. So in honoring your pastor, you honor Jesus, the Giver of that gift. *He* is the One who will reward you.

Actually, the pressure to send out thank-you notes can be a real bondage for a pastor's wife. That's why I don't expect any. But some Christians collect thank-you notes like Boy Scouts collect badges! There almost seems to be a competition to see who can get the most. That doesn't show a true servant's heart. Servants never ask, "What's in it for me?" before they agree to serve.

As I said earlier, many wonderful blessings are connected to serving your pastor. As you serve him and his family, your ability to walk in agape love will grow. Your ability to receive from your pastor will increase. God's blessings will flow like a river to you. You see, you are sowing good seed when you bless your pastor — seed that will produce a rich harvest as God multiplies and returns those blessings back to you.

Blessing Your Pastor
With Your Finances

Blessing your pastor financially is an important part of honoring him. For instance, I once noticed that my pastor's youngest daughter was wearing sandals in October. I asked her mother if the little girl just liked sandals or if she didn't have any other shoes. Her mother said she'd just gone through a growth spurt and had outgrown all her shoes. They were believing God for new shoes for their daughter.

I was appalled that the family of God's gift to me would be in need. I asked the pastor's wife what kind of shoes her daughter wanted. Then I took the child out and bought her two pairs of new shoes — a casual pair for school and a pair of dress shoes.

Maybe somewhere in the world there are pastors who are irresponsible with money, but I haven't come across any. (And it isn't my job or yours to judge anyway. God can take care of that aspect of a pastor's life as well.) Pastors' wives are often experts at getting $1.50 out of every $1.00. But I have seen churches that are just stingy, pure and simple. It's a dishonor to God that some ministry gifts live in poverty and lack, and it should be an embarrassment to the Church.

The world doesn't want to follow leaders in economic want. People would be appalled if the President of the United States lived the way many pastors do.

Imagine our president representing America to the world with holes in his shoes and a ten-year-old beater car! We wouldn't want that for our president, so why would we want that for our pastor? Our president is only an elected official. He is here today and gone in four to eight years. But our pastor is a gift from God.

First Corinthians 9:11-14 is pretty clear about financially supporting the pastor:

> **If we have sown spiritual things for you, is it a great thing if we reap your material things?**
>
> **If others are partakers of this right over you, are we not even more? Nevertheless we have not used this right, but endure all things lest we hinder the gospel of Christ.**
>
> **Do you not know that those who minister the holy things eat of the things of the temple, and those who serve at the altar partake of the offerings of the altar?**
>
> **Even so the Lord has commanded that those who preach the gospel should live** [not just subsist] **from the gospel.**

Ministers are entitled to the abundant life. We have seen where God says they are entitled to *double* honor. Also, consider this: As the leader of the local church, the pastor is supposed to lead the congregation by instruction and example. If he doesn't model abundance, how are the people going to learn to walk in it?

So look around your church. Does your pastor live in abundance? Does the congregation? Do you? Do you see any changes that need to be made?

Many Christians think that if they give money to their church, they are entitled to say how it is spent. But the tithe — ten percent of their increase — is not theirs. It belongs to God.

And all the tithe of the land, whether of the seed of the land or of the fruit of the tree, is the Lord's. It is holy to the Lord.

Leviticus 27:30

"Will a man rob God? Yet you have robbed Me! But you say, 'In what way have we robbed You?' In tithes and offerings."

Malachi 3:8

We aren't entitled to say how our tithe is spent. Therefore, the corporation board that sets the pastor's salary should be comprised of overseers or other ministers, not church members.

Just give your money to your church and let it go. Determine to trust your pastor with it. If that's difficult for you to do, maybe Jesus isn't the Lord of all your life. Jesus wants all of you. He wants to be Lord of your wallet.

There are other ways to financially bless our pastor and his family. We can bless them with gifts of money from us personally. Sometimes these gifts can be for special occasions, such as birthdays, anniversaries, or Christmas. We can also bless them when *we* get blessed financially. We can give them part of our bonuses. We can be open to give anytime the Holy Spirit leads.

When we give of our finances, we give our pastor a double blessing. First, he is blessed financially. Second, he is also blessed because we honor him and recognize his office. It also brings a double blessing to us. The money is a seed for which we can expect a return. We also reap a spiritual return for our obedience.

Some people have a problem giving directly to the pastor because this type of gift is not tax-deductible. Such people are shortsighted. They underestimate God, hiding their greed in the guise of stewardship. But being led by the Holy Spirit regarding where and how to give is the essence of stewardship.

Second Kings 4:8-37 tells the story of a Shunammite housewife. She had her husband build a spare room for Elisha. She had no hidden agenda; she just wanted to bless the man of God. Read the story. She received the desire of her heart — a son — just because she wanted to show honor to God's minister.

Incredible blessings are also available to us as we bless our pastor. Look at what Galatians 6:6-10 says:

Let him who is taught the word share in all good things with him who teaches.

Do not be deceived, God is not mocked; for whatever a man sows, that he will also reap.

For he who sows to his flesh will of the flesh reap corruption, but he who sows to the Spirit will of the Spirit reap everlasting life.

And let us not grow weary while doing good, for in due season we shall reap if we do not lose heart.

Therefore, as we have opportunity, let us do good to all, especially to those who are of the household of faith.

This scripture promises these pastors a return. But how will the return come?

Think of the blessings you have received. How have they come to you? Blessings and increase come through other people, whether through promotions at work, raises, or gifts from others. Therefore, a pastor's congregation is one source God will use to bring him his return.

The way we treat our gift directly affects our life with God. When we take care of our pastor, we honor God. When we judge, control, belittle, or disobey our pastor, we dishonor God. That's why Hebrews 13:17 (*KJV*) says, *"Obey them that have the rule over you, and submit yourselves: for they watch for your souls, as they that must give account, that they may do it with joy, and not with grief: for that is unprofitable for you."*

If we aren't willing to honor our pastor, we may as well not have one. He will be unprofitable for us because he won't be able to fulfill his scriptural functions. Through our own disobedience, we have prevented him from supernaturally pastoring us in a way that brings us to full spiritual maturity.

Offenses, Gossip, and 'Dear Pastor' Letters

Offenses usually come two ways in regard to our pastor: 1) The pastor preaches a sermon we don't like; or 2) A relationship issue causes conflict. If the pastor's sermon is scriptural, it is up to us to make the correction. Remember, the pastor's job is to correct us as necessary. God is using him to mature us. Therefore, if our hearts are open to God, we will quickly make the needed changes our pastor points out.

Relationship issues are more difficult to handle. When I face a conflict in my relationship with my pastor, I try to look at the situation from all points of view. The temptation is to think that the pastor has been inconsiderate. But I take the time to review the conflict or situation, separating it into two parts — what my pastor may have done wrong and what I have done wrong. Once I discover my part in the conflict, my pastor's part doesn't seem that big anymore.

Love covers a multitude of sins (Prov. 10:12). The God-kind of love doesn't seek its own way, nor does it ever fail (1 Cor. 13:5,8). So no matter what relationship issue arises with your pastor, just determine to walk in love. Forgive and forget.

We have to face the awful truth. Sometimes we just want our own way. Sometimes our pride is hurt. But our distress over a conflict with our pastor may be the very thing that reminds us to root out that pride.

Obedience gets easier with practice. So when offense comes, just don't invite him in. If you love God and His Word, you will not be easily offended.

Psalm 119:165 (*AMP*) says it is possible to live free of offenses: *"Great peace have they who love Your law; nothing shall offend them or make them stumble."* This scripture indicates that people who are easily offended are not very mature. It also indicates that mature Christians do not get offended.

So if you have an issue with your pastor, don't tell anyone. Go to the pastor and talk to him privately. Gossip is sin. No one else needs to know. Most matters are easy to resolve when they are kept private. The more people who become involved, the bigger the problem gets.

People who gossip about offenses are really looking for support. They want others to affirm their right to be offended. Once you take a stand and disagree with them, you will stop getting calls from people wanting to rehearse their grievances.

Gossip can be couched in the most spiritual vocabulary: "Pray for me; I'm going to see the pastor. It's nothing — just a little problem."

If it's nothing, why mention it? Words kill! The Bible says, *"Death and life are in the power of the tongue..."* (Prov. 18:21). Loose words destroy unity. Therefore, don't listen to gossip or evil reports about your pastor. Gossip has the power to destroy churches. It needs to be confronted and eliminated from the congregation as soon as it rears its head.

If someone wants to tell you a story they heard or a problem that someone else has, stop them. If someone wants to tell you a grievance, don't listen. Just ask if he has spoken to the other person about it. If the story is hearsay, tell him you don't want to know. Word will get around until rumor-spreaders will stop coming by your door.

Look at what Proverbs 18:19 (*AMP*) has to say about people who continually get offended: *"A brother offended is harder to be won over than a strong city, and [their] contentions separate them like the bars of a castle."* So don't waste your time trying to patch things up with people like that. It probably won't work. Even if it does work, they'll find something new to be offended about tomorrow. Loving God's Word is the only thing that makes people "offense-proof."

Don't listen to someone's grievance so you can report back to the pastor either. The pastor doesn't need to know. It only tears him down to hear the gossip that's currently in circulation. If the pastor confronts a rumor, the one spreading it will probably deny it. Rumor-spreaders are cowardly. If they wanted to do right, they wouldn't listen to rumors in the first place. Whenever they had an issue with the pastor, they would follow scriptural guidelines and deal with it directly.

Also, never, never, *never* write a "dear pastor" letter. The Bible says to confront others in love. Writing a negative letter is not an example of loving confrontation. Love is kind. It cares about the person being confronted. Love isn't rude, nor does it seek its own.

Once a letter is in the mail, that letter has a life of its own. It is out of your control. You have no way of knowing if the recipient even reads it, nor do you have any control over the effect that letter will have on him or her. I have personally seen pastors devastated by these types of letters.

Disgruntled believers often say that a letter to the pastor brings closure to some negative incident. However, it only brings closure to the incident for them. The pastor may feel badly about the letter for some time to come.

Biblical, loving confrontation is a process. It involves going personally to the person who has offended you and talking through the matter with them. So if it helps to get your thoughts in order, go ahead and write a letter. However, once the letter is written, deliver it in person and read it to the pastor.

People who write letters don't want to discuss or solve a problem; they want to get their point across. They don't care how much the pastor gets hurt. These people are interested in one thing — being right. They aren't walking in the God-kind of love that doesn't seek its own. They just want their own way.

Another way disgruntled Christians assert themselves is through "ambushes." This is how it happens: A church member feels that the pastor has some problem and that he has the answer. Either the pastor needs to repent, or the church member has a teaching tape or book that will show the pastor the error of his ways. So the church member takes the materials to church and gives them to the pastor before the service starts.

This is an ambush because the pastor doesn't know it's coming. The believer wants his own way. He isn't concerned that he may be breaking into the flow of the anointing. He just wants his way. The pastor usually takes the materials and then tries to refocus on the service.

This is my rule: I only give the pastor tapes or books that I feel will encourage or edify him. Any personality or people-skills problem the pastor may have is between him and God. My job is to pray.

I also remind myself that the pastor is God's gift to me. My gift doesn't have to be perfect. He is a gift from Jesus, and that is enough for me. I concentrate on being as supportive as I can and receiving all God has for me. I want to be a good and faithful servant who helps my pastor reach the world for Jesus.

Chapter 5
When People Leave

From that time many of His disciples went back and walked with Him no more.

— John 6:66

When believers don't honor their pastors as the Bible commands, the consequences can be devastating. Too often such rebellious behavior results in a difficult situation in which people decide to leave the church. Sometimes it can even cause a church split.

To understand church splits, it's necessary to understand how influence works. Influence is the ability to affect the character, beliefs, or actions of another.

People we admire have a certain amount of influence in our lives. We may be impressed by someone's money, education, spiritual gifts in manifestation, wisdom, or position. Leadership also carries a certain amount of influence with it. People with influence can use that influence to help others, or they can use it for their own purposes.

The Influence of an Offended Leader

When leaders who are in a position to influence others become disgruntled, several things happen at once. For instance, suppose one of the church leaders becomes offended by something the pastor did. The leader may tell others about the offense or just indicate that something is wrong. Gossip-spreaders then try to fill in the blanks to explain why the leader is not his usual self. That starts the rumors.

The offended leader may decide it's time for a change. He steps down from his leadership position and starts visiting other churches. People who are influenced by that person become hurt and bewildered. They can't understand what the problem is. Some have had more personal contact with this leader than with the pastor. These people may start to question the pastor's ability. "How could such a godly person become offended?" they ask. "There must be something more to this situation."

Eventually the offended leader leaves the church. Others in the leader's circle of influence are grieved. Remember, a church is a local body of believers. When a person loses a finger or a hand, he tends to miss it. In the same way, when an important part of that local body is lost, the people feel real pain and grief.

Part of the grief process is anger, which can easily be directed at the pastor in this kind of situation. Isn't everything that happens in a church ultimately the pastor's fault? No, everything is *not* the pastor's fault. He is responsible to do what God tells him to do. When someone leaves, that person is responsible for his decision. Every believer is accountable for the choices he or she makes.

Devastation and Grief

When a leader leaves a church, his or her entire circle of influence sometimes leaves with him. The people who are left are thrown into grief. Now a body that initially lost a finger has lost an arm. The church is devastated. The pastor and his family suffer the most. That's absolutely true — the pastor and his family suffer the most.

The pastor starts to question every aspect of his ministry. He asks himself over and over, *Why?* For a pastor, losing a leader can be as difficult as losing a member of his family. Perhaps he poured his life into that leader, helping him grow and develop in leadership. The pastor's children may have been friends with the leader's children. The pastor may have tried to go after the leader or some of the others who left with him. All this often causes a real spirit of grief to settle over a pastor and his church. It can even affect his home life.

In John 6, Jesus experienced a "church split." He told the multitude about the Bread of Life, and they couldn't handle it (vv. 26-58). Jesus was perfect. He never sinned. His timing was never off. He never got in the flesh. He always walked in agape love. Yet John gives the impression that not only did the Jews complain about Him (v. 41), but many of His disciples left Him at that time (v. 66). It seems that in the end, only the twelve were left: *"...Jesus said to the twelve, 'Do you also want to go away?'"* (v. 67).

The New Testament uses the word "multitude" to describe the crowds who followed Jesus during His earthly ministry. Yet there were only 120 left in the ministry on the Day of Pentecost. After Jesus had ministered for three years and performed so many miracles *"...that even the world itself could not contain the books that would be written"* (John 21:25), only 120 disciples were left waiting for the Holy Spirit as Jesus had commanded before He ascended on High (Acts 1:15).

Recovery

If people all left the church together during a difficult situation, recovery would be easier for those left behind. However, people usually leave over a period of several months. All of a sudden, you look up and half the church is gone. You begin to wonder if the church will survive. You consider going to a big church where you can hide in the crowd. You wonder if a church is a healthy place to be at all.

Suddenly there aren't enough workers for the children's ministry. Your request for funds for new equipment is turned down. Statements from the pulpit indicate that the church income is down. Things are "tight." Pastor's sermons are more somber. You talk to friends from other churches who say they've heard your church is going through a hard time.

This is *not* the time to abandon ship. This is the time to get out the letter you wrote to yourself when you joined the church. Remind yourself of the reasons you originally knew this pastor was Jesus' gift to you. Encourage yourself in the Lord with those reasons. This man of God needs you now. He needs your encouragement and support. He needs a smiling face at church. He needs generous offerings. He needs your honor. He also needs your prayers more than ever.

You may say, "It sounds like my pastor's needs come first." Yes, in this type of situation, that may be true for a while. Your income is not affected by people leaving the church, but his income *is* affected. You have friends and family outside church, but the church is his life. His family needs to be invited for dinner. He needs someone offering to mow his lawn or to baby-sit his children. He needs to know you are with him for the long haul.

He is still the man of integrity you followed; only circumstances have changed. He may be short-tempered or irritable during this difficult time. But he needs you to show him the kind of love that never fails and doesn't keep a record of wrongs. He also needs to hear that it isn't all his fault.

When we choose not to follow our pastor, it isn't the fault of the man of God. God holds leaders to a higher standard. He will deal with anything wrong that the pastor does. Our job is to follow. Moses wasn't held responsible for the rebellion of the people, nor was Jesus held responsible for the multitude who left Him.

Obedience is a choice with only one standard: Is the command illegal, immoral, or unscriptural? "But there's an easier way." That doesn't count. "It's the wrong timing." That doesn't count either. "I think the pastor missed God." Once again, that doesn't count.

Moses struck the rock in anger when he was supposed to just speak to it. Moses was later disciplined for his disobedience (Num. 27:12-14), but the people still received water. God doesn't hold the people accountable for the pastor's mistakes, and He doesn't hold the pastor accountable for the people's mistakes. He is a just God.

Sometimes both pastors and congregations of small churches feel like failures — like all their work has been for nothing. But God measures success very differently. His criterion for success is this: "Did you do what I told you to do? Did you follow Me?"

We don't have to worry about the ultimate outcome. We can just read the end of the Book. We win! The only element of uncertainty is how many we will take with us.

Only one action will cause you to fail: *quitting*. Quitters never win, and winners never quit. So trust in God. Cast your cares upon Him. Hold fast to God's promise in Isaiah 54:17:

"No weapon formed against you shall prosper, and every tongue which rises against you in judgment

you shall condemn. This is the heritage of the servants of the Lord, and their righteousness is from Me," says the Lord.

Then determine that no matter what anyone else in your church does, you will be faithful to honor your pastor and *never quit*!

Chapter 6
The Church in Power

"Most assuredly, I say to you, he who believes in Me, the works that I do he will do also; and greater works than these he will do, because I go to My Father."

— John 14:12

As members of the Church of Jesus Christ, we are supposed to function in power. Acts 1:6-8 states clearly that we are to receive "the Holy Ghost and power" in order to spread the Gospel. Mark 16:17-18 describes the Church operating in power. We're supposed to cast out demons, as well as lay hands on the sick and see them recover.

The Early Church demonstrated this life-changing power. That same anointing of the Holy Spirit and power destroys yokes and lifts burdens today as well (Isa. 10:27). And as we demonstrate the power of God in ministry to others, the world will know we are Jesus' disciples because of the love we show to one another (John 13:35).

This is the Church that can confront the gates of hell and be victorious. But if we cannot be trusted with little, we will not receive more from God. We have already been given five treasures from Him in the form of the fivefold ministry gifts. Of those five treasures, He gives us one very personal gift — our very own pastor. Now He is watching to see whether or not we honor our pastor, for if He cannot trust us with a pastor, how can He trust us with the lost? How can He trust us with real Holy Ghost power? How can He trust us to show the lost His agape love if we cannot love each other?

I hope this book has witnessed to you. If you agree with everything in it, be encouraged. If it has shone light on an area that needs correction, repent. Begin again to honor and truly receive, esteem, welcome, and accept God's gift to you, your pastor. As you treat your pastor with honor and respect, require the same from your fellow believers. Teach new believers about Jesus' gift to them.

As you determine to honor your pastor as God intends, watch the anointing on his life increase. Watch your church become a church of power. Watch those greater works begin to manifest in your church and through you. And watch your own personal walk with God reach a higher level of maturity and abundance than you've ever experienced before!

About the Author

Judy Wilder was saved in 1973 while attending nursing school. Since then, serving God has always been the most important priority in her life. Throughout the past quarter of a century, Judy and her husband George have served together in many areas of helps ministry within their local church, including working as church caretakers and managers of the church book-and-tape ministry. Whatever the need, the Wilders have always endeavored to be available to help their pastor and their church in any way they possibly could.

Judy has also served as a church secretary, a nursery worker, and the coordinator of children's church. In addition, she has worked as a registered nurse for more than twenty years, including three years as a school nurse in a Christian school. Judy and George reside in Aurora, Illinois.

*For additional copies of this book,
please write:*

**Judy Wilder
1718 Garfield Ave.
Aurora, IL 60506
E-mail: judyawild@aol.com**

*Please include your prayer requests
and comments when you write.*